THE AUTUMN OF OUR LIVES

The Life Journey of James Robert Hoffer
Pastor, Missionary, Amateur Radio Operator KW8T

"Weeping may endure for a night,
but joy cometh in the morning."
—Psalm 30:5

"Into every life, some rain must fall."
—Longfellow

JAMES R. HOFFER

All rights reserved. No part of this publication may be reproduced, distributed, or transmitted in any form or by any means, including photocopying, recording, or other electronic or mechanical methods, without the prior written permission of the publisher, except in the case of brief quotations embodied in critical reviews and certain other noncommercial uses permitted by copyright law. For permission requests, write to the publisher, ASPECT Books, at the address below.

Copyright © 2021 James R. Hoffer
Copyright © 2021 ASPECT Books
ISBN-13: 978-1-4796-1386-1 (Paperback)
ISBN-13: 978-1-4796-0750-1 (ePub)
Library of Congress Control Number: 2021903164

All scripture quotations, unless otherwise indicated, are taken from the King James Version (KJV) Public domain.

All scripture quotations, unless otherwise indicated, are taken from the New King James Version® (NJKV). Copyright © 1982 by Thomas Nelson. Used by permission. All rights reserved.

Scripture quotations marked NIV are taken from THE HOLY BIBLE, NEW INTERNATIONAL VERSION®, NIV® Copyright © 1973, 1978, 1984, 2011 by Biblica, Inc.® Used by permission. All rights reserved worldwide.

Holman Christian Standard Bible (HCSB). Copyright © 1999, 2000, 2002, 2003, 2009 by Holman Bible Publishers, Nashville Tennessee. All rights reserved.

The website references in this book have been shortened using a URL shortener and redirect service called 1ref.us, which TEACH Services manages. If you find that a reference no longer works, please contact us and let us know which one is not working so that we can correct it. Any personal website addresses that the author included are managed by the author. TEACH Services is not responsible for the accuracy or permanency of any links.

Published by

www.ASPECTBooks.com

ACKNOWLEDGEMENTS

This book exists today because of the influence of several very special people in my life:

My mother, Lucile, who left each of her four children a wonderful hard cover, 128-page book, handwritten in her beautiful Parker penmanship, recounting her own life experiences just as I have done here in my book. It's a volume I will always cherish. In addition, she left a treasure trove of old letters and pictures that we had written to her over many years. It made our research so much easier.

My sister, Alice, who gave me a helpful book titled *To Our Children's Children—Preserving Family Histories for Generations to Come*.[1] It gets you to thinking and codifying your past, and models the procedures for such a book, as it provides suggestions of topics to write about. She also contributed several important historical details and stories.

My late first wife, Vera, always dedicated to her family, faithful to her calling as a nurse, and supportive of her pastor husband. I miss her deeply.

My children, who corrected some of my recollections and aided with the proofreading, and who enriched this volume with additional stories and suggestions. Their help has been invaluable.

My present wife, Ruth, for her encouragement and nudging to get this project accomplished, which became even more urgent as I faced a health crisis, and who checked over and edited the material and added to my recall.

So, dear folks—Thank you from the bottom of my heart! It took much time and effort, but it turned out to be quite fun and adventuresome, as I pored over those hundreds of letters and photos both old and new.

---

[1] Bob Greene and D. G. Fulford, New York: Doubleday, 1993.

INTRODUCTION

"There is no limit to the usefulness of one who, putting self aside, makes room for the working of the Holy Spirit upon his heart and lives a life wholly consecrated to God. All who consecrate body, soul, and spirit to His service will be constantly receiving a new endowment of physical, mental, and spiritual power. The inexhaustible supplies of heaven are at their command"—Ellen G. White, *Ministry of Healing*, p. 159.

I learned the above marvelous quotation back in a course I took at Columbia Union College, and it has stuck with me ever since. As a human being, I have often faltered in achieving that status, but it has ever been my goal. I am certainly not perfect, nor anyone special, but I believe God has used me and guided me throughout my life and ministerial career.

It is difficult to write an autobiography without constantly employing the first person singular "I", so I hope my readers will understand that it is only given to identify me, and not to give me the credit for anything I have accomplished. The glory and the credit belong to God. I do believe, however, that the many stories and experiences in this little book demonstrate His undeniable guidance, whether through the influence of my parents, family, and friends, my teachers and superiors wherever I have studied and worked, or other circumstances throughout my life.

God has truly blessed me and my family in so many ways. I have had the privilege of traveling to nearly 30 countries and 48 states (Alaska and Hawaii are still on my bucket list), learned several languages, and through amateur radio shortwave my voice has been heard in over 350 countries. My book and other writings have traveled far and wide, and the sermons on my website are still being enjoyed by many. I have become acquainted with thousands and thousands of people, and many hundreds have become close friends.

But no one can ever measure the results in this life. And our most important role is *dedicated Christian*. What joys await us in eternity! And eternity will ever be exciting and full of surprises, as we meet up again with those who mentored us, and those on whom we had a positive influence.

Come now, peek over my shoulder as I share my life with you. And only to God be the glory!

Jim Hoffer

THE AUTUMN OF OUR LIVES

The Life Journey of James R. Hoffer

Pastor, Missionary, Amateur Radio Operator KW8T

THE BEGINNING

It was nearing suppertime over at Jimmy Hoffer's house. He was not home from school. Jimmy's parents were getting very worried. He had never before been this late getting home from school. His mother and dad began to imagine all sorts of bad things. Maybe he had accepted a ride in a stranger's car. Maybe he had run away. Maybe he had hurt himself badly. Mother asked Daddy if he thought they should call the police.... (To be continued.)

My birth certificate affirms that I was born on the morning of April 12, 1940 in Evangelical Deaconess Hospital in Cleveland, Ohio, to Frank J. Hoffer and Ruth Lucile Hoffer. My father's name is listed erroneously with J as his middle initial. It was really F for Ferdinand, a name which he did not like and seldom shared with anyone. My parents' address at the time was 2114 North Avenue in Parma, Ohio. Zip codes did not exist back then. That house apparently still stands, as I found it on Google Earth.

In 1940, a loaf of bread cost 10 cents, a pound of sugar 5 cents, a dozen eggs 33 cents, and a gallon of gas 18 cents. Franklin D. Roosevelt was President. He died on my fifth birthday.

Yes, this is the Cleveland where in 1969 the Cuyahoga River caught fire, due to pollution from the heavy industries around its shores. Cleveland was a major Great Lakes port and steel producer at that time.

Coming to our door regularly were the milkman, the iceman, the meter reader, and the postman. Up and down the street were the ice cream man, the scissors sharpener man, and a Greek man with his produce truck. Door to door went the Fuller Brush man, the Hoover or Electrolux salesman, and others.

My little brother Kenneth William was born on September 19 of the following year but died a few hours later. It was a difficult time for my parents. Mom was not allowed to hold him or ever see him, and she came home to an empty crib and new baby clothes.

My brother William Frank was born on June 11, 1943. When he became old enough, we were buddies and would play a lot together (and fight too, as kids will do).

The early 1940s were war years, and one of my earliest memories is that of going to see one of my uncles off to war at the train station in downtown Cleveland. I was probably three or four then. At that time, the military draft was used by the government to conscript soldiers. Many went into the Army; others chose to enlist in the Navy, Marines, Air Force, or Coast Guard. My uncles Andy (pictured at left) and Roy (pictured on page 85) served. Uncle Bert was a radio engineer for the Voice of America and served in Germany, Morocco, and Okinawa and possibly a few other places. When Dad finally received his draft notice it was the spring of 1945, and because the war ended, thankfully he did not have to go.

Another early memory had to do with a children's radio program in Cleveland. Of course, those were the early years of radio and broadcasts were done live. I was one of the children at the radio studio with perhaps a dozen or so others. As the microphone was held in front of me, I blurted out this wondrous pronouncement: "Haven't I got big knees!" Or so my mother later told me. I guess that was my big break into show business!

My paternal grandfather, Andreas (Andrew) Schwach-hofer, died when I was three, so I never knew him, but he was a fine bricklayer among other trades. Earlier in life he worked at the Winton Motor Carriage Company in Cleveland,[2]  one of the very first auto manufacturers. My grandma, Maria (Mary), loved to bake, and she delighted us often with her cookies, cakes, doughnuts, etc. She had a thick German accent.

They were both native to the Germanic part of Transylvania but didn't know each other over there. Then around 1900 they were part of the great European immigration to the U.S. that occurred in the era of 1880 to 1920. By the boatloads they came to our shores from many countries seeking freedom and work. Andreas and Maria (Weber) actually met in an ethnic club known as Sachsenheim,[3] on Dennison Avenue near downtown Cleveland.

Unfortunately, Grandpa was given to alcohol and there was much trouble in the home. He died at the early age of 64, divorced, homeless, and penniless. I wish I could tell you that Grandma and Grandpa Hoffer had a happy life. But I guess it's better to be honest here. Alcoholism is deadly, and very, very sad. I tell more of their ancestral

---

[2] Picture, 1917 Winton, HymanLtd.com, used by permission.
[3] Sachsenheim (translation: Saxon home) was a club or hall for Germanics. They had dances, parties, and social occasions of all sorts there. Similar clubs sprang up across America to serve other ethnic groups.

story beginning on page 104. We have the genealogical records on my father's side back to 1752.

The wisest man, King Solomon, wrote: "Wine is a mocker, strong drink is raging: and whosoever is deceived thereby is not wise." Proverbs 20:1.

GROWING UP

My parents bought their first house in 1943 for the princely sum of $6,000 and moved in on February 16, 1944. It was located at 12213 Kensington Avenue. Their phone number at first was CLearwater 9435, and later CLearwater 1-9435. (The first two letters were capitalized because they were to be dialed.) They lived in that house for around 40 years! During that time, *many* things happened. Dad and his brother Andy enlarged the house by raising part of the back roof and creating a new bedroom for us boys. During that project, Uncle Andy reached under the table saw to turn it off and cut off a couple of his fingers. They were reattached, but in future years they would always ache in cold weather.

That house at first had a coal furnace. Periodically, the coal man would rumble into the driveway in his noisy truck and deliver a load through the chute into the coal room in the basement. Then I recall Dad with his coal shovel stoking our furnace to keep us all warm. It was hard work, and since the houses were so close, in cold weather our neighborhood was filled with black smoke. Eventually we had natural gas.

Dad and Uncle Andy both worked at Westinghouse Electric Corporation on 58th Street. There were hundreds of employees, and at some point, they joined the Westinghouse bowling league. Dad took us boys along. By now I was in my early teens. I learned to bowl at that time, and now and then when one of the team members was absent, I could bowl in his place. Of course, my score didn't count (for scoring purposes they would just use the missing man's established average to compute the team total), but I got pretty good, once even breaking 200.

Bill and I enjoyed bowling so much that we made our own small bowling alley in our basement. Dad made us a set of pins (I have one somewhere), and we painted lines on the floor. We used a softball to knock 'em down!

I don't remember the year, but I certainly remember the event. Westinghouse had a big Christmas party for their employees, with door prizes. Hundreds of people were present. When the final drawing came down to the grand prize, my parents won! They were awarded a brand-new modern washer and dryer. Wow! What excitement and how timely! With children in the family there was always laundry. And they could get rid of their old wringer washer, and maybe even their clothesline.

Dad also taught me golf. I well remember one time. We borrowed my Uncle Andy's nearly new golf clubs because I didn't have any of my own. One of my shots landed my ball under a tree. I took out an iron (one of the smaller clubs) and gave a mighty swing. I hit the ball okay, but on the upswing the shaft of the club wrapped itself around a branch. Oh, was I mortified! Of course, I did not have any money to pay for it. I guess my Dad paid for a new club. Pictured at left is my almost-hole-in-one in 2014, from 150 yards, hole number 5 at Nob North Golf Course in Cohutta, Georgia.

He also made us a baseball game. It consisted of a plywood table with walls around the field and detailed markings of bases, foul lines, and all the rest. There were carved figures, a batter and a pitcher. He used the plans from one of his favorite magazines, *Popular Mechanics*. He put hours and hours into it.

But one of his incredibly special talents was building model airplanes. This was back in the days of balsa wood, glue, and tissue paper. Some were more utilitarian, and others were museum-quality scale models of warplanes from the two world wars and other times. One was featured on the cover of the *Model Airplanes* magazine, and he displayed frequently at the annual model airplane expo in Toledo, Ohio. He was that good!

Back in my childhood and youth, Dad always built free-flight planes. Once he forgot to set the timer and the plane flew out of sight. But he always put his name and phone number on top. He got a call a few days later from a man who found it in a cornfield in Akron! Much later he got into radio control.

Another of Dad's talents in his earlier life was singing. He had a beautiful operatic tenor voice and could have become quite a singer. I have an old scratchy recording and it is marvelous. Unfortunately, a nagging sinus problem got in the way. And due to his rather introverted personality he never wanted to sing for us. He even took up oil painting at the age of 78. Some of our homes are blessed with his lovely work on our walls.

Mom had a beautiful voice too, and when I was about five years old, she taught me to sing duets with her, using the song "Now Is the Hour." In addition, she was always nurturing and encouraging us, and was a devoted Christian. She kept a pages-long prayer list next to her bed. She took a job at American Greetings in Cleveland to help with our educational bills and was there for many years, and in addition to all that she served as the treasurer for our church. She baked incredible pies and other baked goods, and she considered that an expression of love for her family. (And she always kept the cookie jar full for us kids!) She was the original "people bootie" supplier (knitted slipper) and an amazing seamstress. And she's the one who taught Vera to make sock babies.[4]

---

[4] Pictured on page 115.

One of Dad's favorite friends from work was Earl Simmerer. The Hoffers and Simmerers would often get together. Theresa was wonderful and very crafty. She was always making little things for us. They had no children of their own, so she made us feel very special. Theresa's sister, Rose Giordano, lived with them also. Earl was highly intelligent and techie. He built a Heathkit electronic organ and learned to play it very well. He even had an amateur radio license for a short while.

And oh, the Cleveland Indians! How Bill and I enjoyed attending the games with Dad down at the stadium. In 1948, wonder of wonders, the Indians won the American League pennant and beat the Boston Braves for the World Series. In 1954 they won the pennant again but lost the series to the New York Giants. I cried when Lou Boudreau, beloved third baseman, left the Indians. Later I would come to be a fan of Al Rosen, also a third baseman. In fact, I have his autograph in a scrapbook. Is that why I played third base in college fast-pitch softball?

Other autographs that I accumulated over the years include Rudolph Ringwall, conductor of the Cleveland Symphony Orchestra; Harrison Dillard, Olympic champion runner; singer Glen Campbell, after I translated his song "Less of Me" into Spanish; actor Andy Devine, WB6RER, whom I spoke with by ham radio; humorist Dave Barry, after I sent him a copy of my poem, "It's vs. Its" (See my best poems at the end of this book); actress Sally Field, who played the part of Betty Mahmoody in the movie *Not Without My Daughter*, based on Bill's book of the same name; heroine Betty Mahmoody herself; J. Edgar Hoover; H.M.S. Richards and all the members of the King's Heralds Quartet at that time (early 1950s); and "Uncle" Arthur Maxwell, who wrote the *Bedtime Stories* books.

Personal sightings would include General Douglas MacArthur, in a parade in downtown Cleveland; Richard Nixon, at the back of a campaign train; Senate Chaplain Barry Black, when he preached at my Hagerstown church and we ate lunch together; Dr. Ben Carson, at a book-signing event; General Colin Powell, at a lecture in Benton Harbor, Michigan; Jim and Tammy Faye Bakker (ugh!) at a small Assembly of God church in Laurel, Maryland, many years before he was rich and "(in)famous"; and I had a ham radio contact with Senator Barry Goldwater, K7UGA, and another with Tom Christian, VR6TC, of Pitcairn Island. We also attended an Oral Roberts crusade in a large stadium. Every little while the ushers would stand up with one of his books in their hands while a pitchman on the stage urged us to buy. And after his very lengthy and haranguing sermon, he made a call for people to come forward for healing. It seemed disgusting, just a big show.

But back to my growing-up years. Bill and I loved to walk a mile or so to the nearby Halloran Park, where a baseball diamond beckoned. Often on summer evenings and Sundays several boys would gather, and we would play hardball until it got so dark that we could hardly see the ball! Sometimes we would play baseball in the street in front of our house, and even touch football. I will never forget the time I ran back for a pass, caught the ball, turned around, and ran smack into a fireplug, full in the chest! I fell to the ground, staggered back to our house, and lay on the sofa for the longest time, trying to catch my breath. I never knew whether I had broken a rib. Later in academy I would get into ping-pong, otherwise known as table tennis. As an adult, I won a championship in 2003 in the Hagerstown league.

Our neighbors on the left acquired a television set, and they would invite us over to watch *I Love Lucy* and other programs. Soon we got a TV of our own.

I also got into stamp collecting, big time. I had stamp books filled with stamps from all over the world. That was the beginning of my fascination with geography, which later carried over into my interest in amateur radio. But that is a story for later.

Confession is good for the soul. One afternoon when I was on my way home from Nathaniel Hawthorne public school, my friend Arthur Wall invited me to stop at his house to see his stamp collection. I am sorry to report that when he was not looking, I stole a beautiful stamp from his collection. In later years, when I remembered and regretted this incident, I tried to make amends, but his family had moved, and I had no way to contact him. There are over a hundred Arthur Walls on WhitePages.com, so it would be an impossible task. All I could do was turn it over to the Lord.

I recall many family picnics, most of them at Rocky River Park on the West Side. Back then people did not move around as much. Both sides of my family remained in the Cleveland area for many years. Our picnics were large and included my grandfather Ralph Koeblitz (Mom's father), uncles, aunts, and cousins. I remember playing catch with a baseball with Grandpa, and learning that he was ancient, 70 or so. I would have been in my early teens. It is wonderful belonging to a family with no issues—at least that I am aware of—no jealousies, no unresolved animosities, just love. We always felt love and still do. Of course, like all families, we occasionally had disagreements.

Mr. and Mrs. James were our next-door neighbors on the right. Their sons were Bruce and Larry, and they had a big dog, Major. When I was small, someone asked me where I lived, and I said, "Next to Brucie." So, then they asked, "So where does Brucie live?" I replied, "Brucie lives next to me!"

In 1997, my mother wrote, *"As a child, [Bruce] wanted to grow up to be a garbage man! They used to have open dump trucks and the men on the ground would hand a full can up to the man standing in the stuff. He would empty it and toss the can back. Bruce wanted to be the one on top! He may still get there."*

As a teenager he became interested in printing, so much so that he acquired a small letter press and several fonts of movable type. He canvassed the nearby stores, offering to print for them. He had quite a business going. As an adult he entered the printing business and was quite successful, eventually becoming Public Printer of the United States and CEO of the Government Printing Office, 2002-2006, in Washington, D.C.

(sort of equivalent to Postmaster General). In retirement he and his wife moved to Nevada, where at one point he ran as the Republican candidate for U.S. senator. (He lost.) My neighbor, little Brucie. You never know[5]

Also, a childhood friend from our church, Ron McDermott, became a vice president of the huge Kellogg Corporation in Battle Creek. Gr-r-reat![6]

Our sister Alice was born on October 21, 1948. It was nice to finally have a girl in the family.

Mom and Dad bought themselves a 1948 Studebaker in 1950. The following year we took a vacation trip to New York City to visit Aunt Alice and Uncle Bert. I well remember their huge great Dane dog. He was scary!

On June 8, 1953, the west side of Cleveland suffered a horrible, devastating tornado. We were sitting on our front porch that evening watching the darkening skies when suddenly Dad ushered us down to a safe place in the basement. Our neighborhood was blasted. Of course, the power went off, and soon we could see almost nothing. Our house was mostly spared, but we discovered a two-by-four sticking through our roof, and our garage was leaning several inches to the left.

Devastation was seen for a large portion of our neighborhood. We couldn't venture out because of downed wires, broken glass, and much debris. It was reported that about a block away a baby was picked

---

[5] See https://www.linkedin.com/ in/bruce-james-719957a2.
[6] I snapped this picture at one of Battle Creek's annual hot air balloon festivals.

up by the wind and smashed against the wall of another building. There were a few other deaths. It would be many months before homes and businesses were rebuilt.

Westinghouse went on strike in the fall of 1955, and it lasted 156 days, right during the holiday season! Those were exceedingly difficult days for my parents. Dad took on a few part-time jobs, so desperate that for a time he drove and unloaded a beer truck. It was very humiliating for him, but he had to do something. Grandpa Ralph Koeblitz (at left), Mom's father, also helped us get through it. We are no strangers to hardships.[7]

Our house originally had just one bathroom with a bathtub but no shower. After having gone to summer camp and then academy I learned about the pleasure of taking showers. I asked my father if we could please have a shower somehow. Soon afterward, he surprised the family by building a shower stall in one corner of our basement, near the washing machine, doing all the carpentry and plumbing work himself. It was great but would soon come into play in a tragic story.

In 1956 our house again suffered, this time from a fire that started in our attic on Friday afternoon, May 11. I was down in the basement taking a shower to get ready for the Sabbath. Just at that moment my parents with Alice drove home from shopping, when Dad saw a lot of smoke coming out of an upstairs window. Bill was already outside, but Dad thought I might be upstairs. He ran up the stairs frantically looking for me and, in the process, suffered burns on his face and arms. Finally, he discovered I was not there and found me downstairs. By that time, the fire department had arrived.

All my clothes were lost in the fire. I had taken my pajamas, bathrobe, and slippers down to the basement for the shower, and that was all that was left. Of course, going to church the next day was impossible.

---

[7] We have the Koeblitz side of the family genealogy back to 1782, thanks to the extensive research of our late Uncle William Koeblitz.

Our church family and others rallied around to provide for us. We lived in a rented house up the street for a few months. I still have an old poetry book[8] with smoke marks on it. For a long time, I didn't know how the fire had started. Many years later, in a letter written after our father's death, Bill, age eight at the time, admitted that he caused the fire by playing with matches in the attic. We'll never know why, since he recently passed away.

We enjoyed some very special vacations. One year we drove up to see Niagara Falls. I remember that we also visited the nearby Nabisco Shredded Wheat factory. At the end of the interesting factory tour, they sat us all down to enjoy a free bowl of Shredded Wheat! In 1949, Dad had a summer job of painting someone's vacation cabin at Pymatuning Lake in Pennsylvania. The flies were terrible, so Mom gave each of us boys a fly swatter and an empty Mason jar and promised us a penny for each fly we brought back. Bill and I really went to war on those flies!

Since Uncle Bernie and Aunt Pearl had use of a vacation cabin on Kelley's Island in Lake Erie, one summer (1956) we spent a couple of weeks there, fishing and enjoying life. My cousin Bryan offered to teach me to drive. They kept an old stick-shift car up there, so the lessons began. I soon got the hang of stick shift, but not before mowing down several stalks of corn at the corner of a large field! Now I could drive a car at 16, but Dad wouldn't allow me to get a license until I was 18. Oh, the challenges of being the icebreaker firstborn. My siblings got their licenses at 16!

SCHOOL DAYS

In the fall of 1945, my parents enrolled me in kindergarten at the elementary school[9] on West 130th Street. It would have been about a mile, not fun on bitter winter days. My parents wouldn't own a car for a few years, so we walked back and forth in those early times.

---

[8] H.M.S. Richards, *Have Faith in God.*
[9] Picture, Nathaniel Hawthorne School, courtesy of Aaron Turner, www.oldohio schools.com, used by permission.

In 1986 I wrote this article:[10]

It was a lovely afternoon in early spring, just perfect as two Jimmys left school and headed home. Jimmy Hoffer walked beside his friend, Jimmy Wadsworth. The two Jimmys were in first grade, and they were the best of friends. "Hey," Jimmy Wadsworth said, "why don't you stop at my house for a minute on your way home and see my toys?" "Sure," said Jimmy Hoffer. "That sounds like fun. I've never been to your house before." Of course, Jimmy Hoffer intended to stay for only a few minutes; but as the two Jimmys played in the back bedroom, time flew by.

Meanwhile, it was nearing suppertime over at Jimmy Hoffer's house. Jimmy Hoffer was not home from school. His parents were getting very worried. Jimmy had never before been this late getting home from school. His mother and dad began to imagine all sorts of bad things. Maybe he had accepted a ride in a stranger's car. Maybe he had run away. Maybe he had hurt himself badly. Mother asked Daddy if he thought they should call the police.

It was also suppertime back at the Wadsworth home. Mrs. Wadsworth did not know that Jimmy Hoffer was in her house. When she went to the bedroom to call her Jimmy to supper, she was very surprised to see another Jimmy there!

"Why, Jimmy," she said to her Jimmy, "you didn't tell me you brought a friend from school home with you."

"I'm sorry, Mom," said Jimmy Wadsworth. "This is my friend from first grade. His name is Jimmy Hoffer."

"Hello, Jimmy," Mrs. Wadsworth said. "But do your parents know you are here?"

"Well, uh," stammered Jimmy Hoffer, "I guess not. I really didn't mean to stay this long."

"Well, now!" Mrs. Wadsworth understood how worried Jimmy Hoffer's mother and father must be. She said, "We had better telephone your home right now!" And she did.

But now it was too dark outside. Neither family owned a car, for this happened many years ago. Mrs. Wadsworth told Jimmy Hoffer's

---

[10] *Our Little Friend*, March 14, 1986, slightly adapted.

parents that he could spend the night at the Wadsworth house. Little Jimmy Hoffer was frightened when he tried to eat strange food in that strange house and rest that night in a strange bed. Sleep did not come to him easily.

Next morning, Jimmy Hoffer's mother came to get him and walk him home. It seemed like a long walk, for not much was spoken, not just then.

That evening, when Jimmy Hoffer's daddy came home from work, can you guess that Jimmy got a good talking-to? And can you guess what else happened?

I know exactly what happened, for I am Jimmy Hoffer. Never again did I go somewhere without my parents' permission. And you'd better not go anywhere without your *parents' permission!*

I guess I always liked girls. There were those pretty, blonde twin girls in kindergarten, Jean and Jane Burger. I always wondered what happened to them. Later in fifth grade there was Jackie Kopec, who lived just a couple of blocks away from me. I tried to befriend her but no luck. I probably looked pretty nerdy (a word that did not exist in 1949) back then. In fourth grade I was having difficulty reading the blackboard during classes, so the teacher counseled with my mother about having my eyes examined. That's when I began to wear glasses, at the age of nine. Ugh! But eventually I got used to it.

It was in this elementary school that I took violin lessons and learned tap dancing. Neither activity came to be a part of me.

Walking home from school one warm and sunny autumn afternoon, I happened to pass under a large maple tree, dropping its seeds one by one, like miniature helicopters spiraling to the ground. I was probably about eight or nine years old at the time. I picked one up and dropped it, watching it fall and admiring its design. I put it in my pocket.

That evening, when Dad came home from work, I asked him if I could plant it. He said yes and found a clear place in the flower garden for it. I worked up a little spot in the dirt and planted it, with the seed part in the ground and the little tail sticking up. Lo and behold, in about a week it took root and sprouted. After a few weeks it was well established and growing.

A few months later it was about three feet tall and would soon be crowding out the flowers, so Dad and I transplanted it to a spot in the middle of the lawn, about two-thirds of the way back from the house. There it stayed for many years.

Time passed, and I was grown up and married. Now the tree was so large, about 30 feet tall, that it absolutely dominated our back yard! One time when I was home, Dad said, "Jim, I'm sorry but the maple tree is way too large now, and we are going to have to cut it down." Not only was it too big for our tiny back yard, only 40 feet wide, but it had a double trunk and was really not very attractive.

A double trunk! If we had taken care of that when it was a baby tree, cutting off the extra trunk when it was small, the tree would have righted itself and been more attractive. Just so, bad habits and notions must be pruned early, or they take over our lives. It was a good lesson for me to learn.

CHURCH AND CHURCH SCHOOL

In 1947 my parents became Seventh-day Adventist Christians. I was only seven at the time, but here is how it happened. My mother was nominally a Jehovah's Witness, since her mother and older brother were strong in that belief. But Mom was only 13 when her mother died, so the JW influence was somewhat less. Dad was raised Adventist but left the church in his late teens. Regarding Mom's parents, her father, Ralph Koeblitz, had a brother Ed and a sister Clara. During their teens, they made a pact to never get married. But when Ralph met Sina Pearl Ensign he fell in love.

They were married on September 23, 1908. By the way, we have the Ensign genealogy back to a James Ensign, born in England in 1607. He may even have been related to King James! So much for the pact!

Our neighbors, the James's, invited us boys to go with them to Sunday school, since we weren't attending church anywhere at the time. However, one day we came home telling about how that bad people were going to burn in hell when they died, and that turned out to be a wake-up call for our parents. That got my parents to thinking, so they decided to try attending Grandma Mary Hoffer's church (pictured below), since Adventists and Jehovah's witnesses have similar views on the state of the dead. More on that topic later.

That one decision, as it turns out, had a profound influence on my life. They chose to join the Adventist church in Lakewood, Ohio and were baptized by immersion, after taking Bible studies from Eva Bruder. So was Alice—she was in Mom's tummy at the time! And from that time forward, I could count on hearing the King's Heralds quartet singing "Lift Up the Trumpet" from our AM radio at 9:30 every Sunday morning, the wonderful messages from speaker H.M.S. Richards, the closing strains of "Near to the Heart of God" and Pastor Richard's ongoing poem, "Have Faith in God."

Shortly afterward, in fifth grade, I was enrolled in the Lakewood church school, which had about 50 students at the time. The teachers were Frank and Letha Fuller. About a year later I was baptized by our pastor, Erwin Lehnhoff, on December 22, 1951.

I was 10 years old when my parents first sent me to summer camp. As I recall, six boys and a counselor occupied each cabin. That first year one of my cabinmates was Bruce Ashton. Later Bruce and I were classmates at Mount Vernon Academy and graduated together. Bruce was an excellent pianist even at a young age. He went on to become the head of the Music Department at Southern Adventist University in Collegedale, Tennessee, for some 35 years. More about Bruce later.

Eventually I attended summer camp at Tar Hollow five times, missing only the year of our house fire. I will never forget the evening campfires and many of the songs and rounds we would sing. How about "Rheumatism, rheumatism, how it pains, how it pains, up and down the system, up and down the system, when it rains, when it rains," to the tune of "Frère Jacques"? And the annual camp meetings put us in touch with some of the best speakers in the church, such as H.M.S. Richards, Sr. himself. We will never forget the rows and rows of army tents where we stayed and sweated on hot summer nights. In 1951 they had to cancel camp meeting after a few days because of sanitary system problems. Everyone was getting sick with dysentery.

Some years later, Paul Horton (sitting on the lower bunk) and I would be on the giving end, pastoring churches in Ohio, being teachers at summer camp, pitching tents at camp meeting, and directing children's departments there, leading the next generation to Jesus.

Some of the friends I made at Lakewood became friends for life. Among them was Gerda Schmidt. Gerda was new to America, having been born in Germany. We had a good time helping her along with her English, including several good laughs.

I think back to that wonderful church school library, full of inspiring pioneer missionary stories; to our godly teachers and the Bible lessons through all levels of education; and to the lifelong friends we made along the way. Sadly, some of those friends have passed on, and some have left the faith of their childhood. But many of us have remained true, and up into our later years still cherish our Adventist educational experience. Regardless of a few spiritual bumps and jolts along the way, we prefer to minimize the effect of human frailty and focus on the big picture and the great reward awaiting us.

Back then the Adventist churches had a fall fund charity drive known as Ingathering. Each church was assigned a monetary goal and was expected to reach it. Between Thanksgiving and Christmas, we would be out on the streets, singing carols and soliciting door to door for donations for mission and relief work. One older man insisted on taking along his saxophone, but the cold weather made the notes sound rather sour. We always stifled a groan when that man was assigned to our singing band. Despite the sometimes-bitter winter winds off Lake Erie, and sometimes heavy snows, we always seemed to make our goal.

Now let me tell you some more about Paul Horton. Paul was six months younger than I, and a grade behind, but we became fast friends, often visiting each other in our respective homes. He had moved to Cleveland with his family from Savannah, Georgia, and for a while his southern accent persisted. At first, he seemed to have some prejudice against blacks. Later he became a missionary to Africa of all places, and I will never forget the picture he sent back with his arm around a black person. God is so good. He takes us as we are, but He doesn't leave us that way.

My brother Dennis was born on July 11, 1954. Looking back to those years of our childhood, we remember that games and puzzles were a big part of the Hoffer household. Dad would play marbles with us, but the board games and puzzles, he left to Mom, who loved them like we did. Dennis, like all the rest of us, learned counting, spelling, reading, (and taking turns!) from the games Mom used to play with us when we were preschool kids. Parcheesi in particular gave us early math and counting skills. Later, Dennis and Alice played a lot of Risk, Chinese Checkers, and Battleship, which we would hand draw on graph paper. Reading skills came from Scrabble, the *Little Friend* magazine Mom read to us nightly, and the weekly load of library books from our every-Friday trip to the Eastman Branch library at Lorain and W. 117th near Kroger's, the Robert Hall clothing store, and Harry Oif's shoe store where we always got our Sabbath shoes. We still remember the big wooden podium-like foot X-ray box that you could stand on and stick your feet into. Wonder how much excess radiation we soaked in from that! Often, Mom would stick Dennis in the buggy, and we would take turns pushing him all the way there and back!

MOUNT VERNON ACADEMY

Our little school went only through the tenth grade, so it became necessary for us to transfer to an Adventist boarding school, Mount Vernon Academy in Mount Vernon, Ohio, to finish high school. Paul and I roomed together in the boys' dorm, along with another friend from the Cleveland area, Wayne Westfall. The school had a work/study program, so we had to work a certain number of hours in some school industry, or be a teacher's reader, or whatever. I chose to work in maintenance and learned an awful lot about fixing windows and doorknobs, making minor plumbing repairs, etc. I was even trusted to make repairs in the girls' dorm. Along with wonderful dedicated Christian teachers and Professor Jack Shull as principal, it was a very formative part of my life.

I enjoyed being part of the academy choir, with Charles Pierce directing. I also took French horn for a while but was never very good at it. My roommate, Paul, played the guitar, so I learned from him. Then one day I heard an accordion from across the hall. It was Leroy Snider. I knocked and entered and asked him to teach me. He replied that he would if I would teach him guitar. And we did just that.

Our class had a pizza party on the evening of November 19, 1957 and in the morning (Mom's birthday), I woke up with terrible pains on one side. I was rushed to the hospital, where they discovered that my appendix was almost ruptured! Surgery was scheduled immediately. During recovery, my visiting "friends" would deliberately crack jokes to try to make me laugh, and oh, the pain I had in my stitches!

I dated many girls during my two years at Mount Vernon Academy, but no serious relationship was formed. Fortunately, God had someone better for me, as I would soon find out.

COLUMBIA UNION COLLEGE

During the summer of 1958, as I was preparing to head for Washington Missionary College in the fall, I wasn't quite sure what courses I wanted to take. My father, who never finished high school but who was highly skilled in mechanical drawing and careful workmanship, aspired for me to go into engineering. But God had other ideas. One afternoon as I was seated at the kitchen table and leafing through the college course catalog, my mother, who was at the sink across the room doing dishes, remarked, "Jimmy, have you ever thought of being a minister?" I don't recall responding verbally, but something in my mind resonated. From the age of 14 or so I had begun reading my Bible from cover to cover as well as the Conflict of the Ages series by Ellen White. Checking out the Religion Department section of the catalog, I became more and more excited, as so many of the course titles appeared remarkably interesting to me. This was obviously God's call, and yet in later years Mom didn't remember it happening quite that way. So, in September, off I went to college in Takoma Park, Maryland.

It would turn out to be a five-year experience since I had to work my way through. Again, I was assigned to the Maintenance Department. Later I was a teacher's office assistant, first with Professor Linnie Keith of the English Department (who thought I should change to being an English major), and then with Dr. Leslie Hardinge of the Religion Department. Dr. Hardinge became a friend and mentor, with his love for the topic of the ancient Hebrew sanctuary and all its symbolism. Together we assembled his book *Shadows of His Sacrifice*, which back then meant that someone typed up a draft, which would later be corrected by cutting and pasting words and letters as needed here and there, to then being assembled and photocopied or mimeographed into the final product. As he handed me a copy (I still have it.), he quoted his rationale for donating it to me: "Thou shalt not muzzle the ox that treadeth out the corn." (1 Timothy 5:18, KJV). I worked for Dr. Hardinge for two school years, and that was the spark that led me to write my own book on the sanctuary in 2014.

Here I must interject an experience in 1959, the summer after my freshman year. I had made a special friend that year in college, John Patrick, a new Adventist from near Charleston, West Virginia. He was planning to spend the summer working as a "colporteur" or literature evangelist, canvassing homes and selling Christian books and Bibles door to door. So we took the training, and he invited me to stay at his house in Standard, West Virginia, near Charleston. When Dad drove me down there, a very long drive in those days from Cleveland (no interstates), he commented, seeing the tiny post office there, that he and Mom had better not send any packages, as they wouldn't fit in the post office!

Standard appeared to be like a sandwich. Built in a "holler" (hollow) as they said down there, it was sandwiched between two high ridges, with a creek, Paint Creek, a railroad bed, a row of houses, a road, and another row of houses. The next "holler" over was Cabin Creek, the home of the famous basketball player, Jerry West, with whom John had gone to high school. One day as we were swimming in the creek, a dead chicken floated by! And I discovered that John's father, Claude, had his own whiskey still in the basement. West Virginia was surely different! John's younger sister, Patty, was kind of pretty, but like so many West Virginians, she already had a tooth or two missing.

John's pastor at Charleston was Glenn Sharman and the publishing director was Leonard Bierlein. John's hard-working mother, Mary, served us grits and eggs for breakfast, unlike the Cheerios I was used to at home. John was the eighth of 12 children!

We made several interesting contacts, but since it was a poor year for the coal mines around there, few people had extra money to spend on books. While it was a great experience, we did not do very well financially. When I called my father, he made that long drive down from Cleveland again to take me back home. (Oh, how we sacrifice for our kids!) For part of the remainder of the summer I sold wooden engraved name and house number signs to residents of trailer parks in the Detroit area with another friend, Chuck Fryling. The following couple of summers Dad got me a job with my cousin Bob Lorig, working at his tent and awning rental business. So again, I was "canvassing"! By the way, John and I have remained friends through the years, and for the last few summers we have often gone golfing together.

Dr. William Loveless was at that time the young and flamboyant associate pastor of Sligo church. Bill Loveless had no problem driving his convertible around Takoma Park or being seen on the campus in Bermuda shorts. While he may have shocked some of the older members, he was greatly beloved by the students. Bill and I actually became friends, and in later years whenever he saw me, he would call me Jimmy. Dr. Loveless had a keen and perceptive mind. As we went through *The Desire of Ages* in the class on the life of Christ I took from him, he would have us highlight passages that brought out great principles, and we would often discuss these.

During my second year, I got way behind financially. Of course, the previous summer had not gone very well, and my parents were not able to help much. I was called into the treasurer's office and told that if I did not come up with some money, I would have to leave school. I shared my distress with Dr. Hardinge, and he went into action for me. He found some funds somehow, and together with money from Neal Wilson, president of the Columbia Union, and Dr. Loveless, my school year was saved. All those individuals are long-gone now, but I will never forget them.

About halfway through my college experience, the college's name was changed to Columbia Union College. It is now Washington Adventist University.

I had always loved singing, so I joined the choir, as I had done in academy. Then four of us formed a quartet, the Echoes: Julio Cestero, tenor; Dick Brown, second tenor; I as baritone; and Vernon "Butch" Tompkins, bass. We often performed for school events. We even perfected the complicated song "Mr. Sandman" totally by ear.

Butch was a sort of free spirit. He had a great bass voice but didn't attend church much. One Sabbath afternoon he walked the 10 miles down to the Washington Monument in D.C., skipped the elevator, walked all the way to the top and back down again, and all the way back to the campus. He did not return to school the following year. Instead, he turned his back on religion and joined the Navy. We had no contact then for about 50 years. In 2009 we found an address for him through a relative in his hometown of Grand Rapids, Michigan. He was now living in Kissimmee, Florida. Vera and I were in that area and decided to drop in to see him impromptu. He hesitated but let us in briefly. He was nothing but a shadow of his former buoyant self. He had taken up smoking and drinking in the service and lived a loose life. He was very emaciated and part of one arm was missing. Not long afterward we heard he had passed away. Oh, it could have been so different! Why do people rebel against God like that? We took some pictures, but I can't bring myself to show them here.

I dated several girls in college, but God had something special waiting for me the summer of 1960. An evangelism project called "Voice of Youth" involved young folks like us in holding public meetings and presenting Bible topics. The church rented a high school auditorium in Berea, Ohio, and put out advertising. Prior to that there were training sessions at our Lakewood church. One of my friends there, Carol Ronay, invited her friend Vera Poguljsky, from another Adventist church in the area, to join her for this project. She introduced me to Vera, and that started our friendship. That evening after sunset a roller-skating party was held in the school gym, and Vera and I skated around and around. The rest of that summer we spent many hours on the phone, took many bus trips back and forth across town, and enjoyed much time on the nearby tennis court, where somehow the score was always "love." Well, she had plans to attend a different college in the fall, but it didn't take long to persuade her to change to Columbia Union College.

GOLDEN RULE DAIRY

About this same time my roommate, John Adams, had taken on an off-campus job, delivering milk for Golden Rule Dairy, owned by an Adventist family. Basically, it was a bottling plant, buying the milk from farmers. John said that the wages were surprisingly good, so I interviewed and signed up too. It involved getting up around midnight, stopping at Horn & Horn restaurant for an early breakfast, heading out to the plant, then loading our trucks with milk (regular, chocolate, supreme), cottage cheese, eggs, etc. At holiday time we carried nonalcoholic eggnog also. Then we would head out on our routes all over the Takoma Park and Silver Spring (Maryland) areas.

The trucks weren't refrigerated, so in warm weather we had to carry large amounts of ice. The dairy provided insulated boxes for the people's porches. One of my routes had around 500 customers!

Back in those days milk came in glass bottles, so we had to retrieve the empties from the porch box and insert the fresh products. Once in the semi-darkness of the morning I tripped and fell over an unseen little fence and severely cut my hand on broken glass. I had to go to an emergency room at a nearby hospital for some stitches.

In winter we had to use chains on our rear tires. The trucks were manufactured by Divco, and they were stand-up drive. To the right was an accelerator, and to the left the other pedal served first as a clutch and then as a brake, as you pushed down, holding on to the steering wheel.

Another time I had an accident on snowy roads with a potato chip truck in the wee hours of the morning at the intersection of Piney Branch Road and New Hampshire Avenue. The driver and I ate potato chips and drank chocolate milk while we waited for help to arrive,

One holiday season when we were carrying the eggnog, I drank way too much of it during my hours of work. Boy, what a bellyache I had when I got home! A nice thing about the holiday season was that we would leave Christmas cards for all our customers, and the next day or two they would leave gifts of money and other things. Once someone left me a bottle of whiskey. Believe me, I poured it down the drain before I got home!

And, oh, those milkman notes, left in the porch box! Because we delivered at night, the customer could call in a special order to the office during the day or leave a note in the box. How dismaying it was to carry a heavy load of milk to the porch, only to find a note that said, "Please, no milk today." I still have some of the more humorous ones in a scrapbook, as follows (all misspellings are theirs):

"Have a cigar from apartment #2. We just got a boy."

"Dear milkman: When we get milk please put a X on the box with this chalk."

"Leave to quarts of milk please."

"Milkman: ½ gal ragler milk, 1 bottle whiping cream. Thanks."

"S 3." (I figured out that he wanted three quarts of skim milk.)

"Please leave extra milk and a doz. eggs. I'm desperate."

"No milk today. We're loaded."

"Milkman, please give us 1 pound butter and 1 dozen eegs." Well, I looked all over my truck and couldn't find any "eegs," so I left her a dozen eggs.

One lady signed her note *"Lots of love, Mrs. M."* Maybe she was trying to entice me. I saw her once through the window, peeking out at me in the wee hours of the morning, but I didn't pay her any attention.

But the best note of all said *"Darling Milkman, please buy bread and empty the garbage. Don't wake me up till 9:15 p.m. Love, Vera."* This was in the spring of 1961, and by now she had her own apartment and happened to be on my milk route in Silver Spring. She worked nights at what was then the Washington Sanitarium.

With the income from my milkman days, I was able to get married, raise a child, and later finish college nearly debt-free in 1963. Eventually the dairy had to close as the land was purchased for one of the interchanges of the new I-495 Washington Beltway.

WEDDING BELLS

I proposed to Vera in the fall of 1960, and soon wedding plans were in the making. Vera's mother was not in favor, but Vera was 18 and of legal age. She announced to her mother that she was getting married even if we had to elope! Mother finally had a change of heart, and everything was fine after that.

We were married on June 18, 1961, at Vera's church on the east side of Cleveland on Euclid Avenue. The officiant was Pastor Bill Bornstein, who many years later confessed that he thought we were pretty young to be getting married and was concerned that it might not last—but it lasted four days short of 55 years.

We didn't have much of a honeymoon, since we got married on a shoestring, so we went to a motel just outside of Cleveland for a couple of nights. It was all we could afford.

On the final day we had a frantic call from her mother. We had not told anyone where we were, so she called all the motels in the Cleveland area looking for us. (Nowadays no motel would have given out personal information.) When we finally connected, she shouted, "You're not married, you're not married!" And Vera assured her that, yes, we were legally married. "But," she exclaimed, "you haven't had the civil ceremony yet!" Then we explained that in the U.S. pastors are legally authorized to perform marriages, not like back in the "old country," Europe. We later learned that this practice is still followed in both countries where we lived in South America, Uruguay, and Brazil, and undoubtedly others. The couple is first married at the courthouse by a justice of the peace, and then comes the wedding blessing at the church, which has no legal standing.

COLLEGE, CONTINUED

We transferred our membership to the large Sligo church on the campus. Further into our college courses, we ministerial students were assigned to one of the other churches in the area to get experience. My assignment was to the Adelphi church. We had a good time practicing our preaching on those poor but gracious folks and learning pastoral visitation. Among our new friends at Adelphi was Jim Morgan, who owned a Texaco gas station. For a while I worked at the station, pumping gas, cleaning windshields, and checking oil. Later he taught me to repair tires, do oil changes and grease jobs, and many other things. This information came in very handy in a few years when we went to the seminary in Michigan, as you will see later in our story.

Vera had been enrolled in the nursing course but having to work and take a full load of classes, she found it difficult to keep up. So, she dropped out of the study part but continued to work as a nurse's aide at the hospital on campus. She would continue as an aide for many years. She was always empathetic and caring, and patients loved her.

One of her patients at the Washington Sanitarium was an older lady who had to give up driving. She gave Vera her old car, a 1951 Kaiser. It was basic transportation, but that was about all. The roof leaked, and when it rained the water would fall into our laps. But it was the first car we ever owned, and now I wouldn't have to beg rides to get to work at the dairy.

We needed to find new living quarters at one point. We answered an ad to rent a basement apartment from none other than Pastor and Mrs. Eric B. Hare, the famous former missionaries to Burma. All was well until we awoke on our very first morning in the apartment. Suddenly, there was a loud scream from Vera. I came running to see what the matter was. The sink was full of roaches crawling everywhere. Then she said, "Honey, I just can't stay here." Sadly, we went upstairs to tell Mrs. Hare and request that our deposit be returned. When she heard that, she put her arm around Vera and said these words: "My dear, you will never make a missionary!"

Fortunately, she was mistaken. Not many years later we went to South America as missionaries.

The following year, on July 2, 1962, Vera finally became a U.S. citizen, being sworn in at the courthouse in Rockville, Maryland along with a large group of others.

On February 13, 1963, we were blessed with the birth of our first daughter, Barbara Jeanne. Vera had earlier been pregnant with twin boys, but they were stillborn at five months. So, this successful birth event was especially delightful.

In our tiny apartment (converted garage) at 903 Domer Avenue, we didn't have much room for pets, but we could have turtles—the small ones you could buy at the dime store. I made a terrarium for our three cute little turtles, Oscar, Samson, and Hercules. One food they enjoyed was small pieces of beef jerky. When they smelled it coming, they picked up their little heads and stared in our direction. Later, we also obtained a parakeet, Perky.

I mentioned earlier that it took five years to complete my college experience, due to finances. But all worked out very well, and during my senior year I was interviewed by several conference presidents. We decided to return to our home state of Ohio. Elder Donald Hunter was the president who called me into the ministry.

ANDREWS UNIVERSITY SEMINARY

After spending the summer of 1963 at my parents' home in Cleveland and visiting with her mother and sister on Detroit Avenue some miles away, we finally headed west to Berrien Springs, Michigan, for seminary. Sometime during that year, we were able to get rid of that 1951 Kaiser and purchase a new Pontiac from an Adventist dealer there.

We received a monthly stipend from our sponsoring Ohio Conference of $195. To supplement that, one of my first endeavors was to try for off-campus work. There were around four service stations in that little town, so I went looking. I stopped at this place and that without any success. Finally, I came to the Standard Oil station at the main downtown intersection. On a Friday afternoon, dozens of customers were lined up, needing gas for the weekend. I asked one of the workers who the boss was, and he indicated a man who was at the pumps working hard to keep up. I went up to him and spoke briefly, but he told me that right then he did not have time to talk. Seeing his predicament, I went to get a squeegee and paper towels and began to clean windshields. Then I asked him if I could check oil and pump gas, and he said yes. By the time things had settled down I had my job! My previous experience at Jim's Texaco in Takoma Park paid off!

We seminary guys would sometimes get up touch football games on the lawn of the Garland Apartments (we lived in B-10). We had a great time. Some of my classmates would go on to important pastoral or teaching positions in the denomination.

Seminary was outstanding! I especially enjoyed my classes with professors Edward Heppenstall, Daniel Augsburger, Earle Hilgert, Steven Vitrano, and Charles Wittschiebe. The final summer 1964 session consisted of tent evangelism directed and taught by Dr. Vitrano. We were involved in a lot of follow-up visitation and preaching in some of the nearby churches. The venue was East St. Louis, Illinois, just across the river from St. Louis, and we had a "bubble tent," held up by pressurized air. The novel structure attracted many people. The famous archway across the Mississippi River was under construction at the time and would open the following year.

The meeting topics came around to presenting what Adventists call "the state of the dead." On the preceding night Dr. Vitrano announced to the audience that on the following evening he would actually present and show a soul. When that time came the next night, he told the audience that this was the very moment he was going to show everyone a soul.

Then he reached behind the curtain, and Vera handed him little Barbie, one year old. "Yes, folks, this is a soul, and you are seeing her with your very own eyes!" From there he went on to explain the true definition of a soul, as given in Genesis 2:7.

After the meetings, we were then officially finished with seminary, attended summer graduation in Berrien Springs, prepared to head for Ohio for a mini-vacation with family, and then on to our first pastoral assignment. All told, we would be in the ministry full-time for 41 years, plus five part-time. Those years included six of mission service in South America.

PASTORAL YEARS

Our first assignment was in the five-church district centered in Athens, Ohio, in the southeastern part of the state. The larger church was at Athens, a university town. Then there were smaller churches in Glouster, Bartlett, Beverly, and Pomeroy. The district pastor was a fine New Zealander gentleman named Frank Gifford with his wife Jean.

Every other Sabbath we would switch our speaking appointments, one Sabbath at Athens and Pomeroy, and the next at Glouster, Bartlett, and Beverly. Our purpose there as an intern was to learn under the oversight of a seasoned pastor. Frank and Jean had served widely in their home country and in islands of the South Pacific, like Fiji. They were very gracious, understanding, and patient as they led us through two years of training and experience. One of our deacons was George Bush (not the president, of course). We would meet up with him again later in life.

We lived in the town of The Plains, just a few miles from Athens, and our address was simply P.O. Box 393. We had room for a nice little vegetable garden, which was a big help. Vera enjoyed working in the garden and later canning and freezing the veggies. I'll never forget the day when a neighbor's pig got out of its pen and was rummaging around in our garden. I have a picture somewhere of a very pregnant Vera chasing the pig!

One afternoon Vera and I decided to visit an inactive member family, the Ruggles, in Beverly, Ohio. After a pleasant visit and our prayer time, Russ, W8VIL, invited me into an adjoining room to show me his ham radio setup. In those days, amateur radios were large and heavy and contained many vacuum tubes. He flicked the receiver on, and soon we began to hear voices from all over. I think I had heard of ham radio before, but this was the first time seeing it up close. He asked if I knew any ham operators, and I remembered my friend Bill Hooker back in Takoma Park (currently WG6A). So, he found an available frequency on  80 meters and put out a call for anyone in the Washington, D.C., area. Soon a person responded, took down the information about Bill, and a short while later there he was, speaking to us from Takoma Park. I was fascinated. Russ sent me home with some phonograph records to learn Morse code, and some books to study.

In about six weeks I was ready for my Novice exam, which Russ could administer. My first call sign was WN8OVC (N for novice). Several months later I received my General class certification, requiring Morse code at 13 words per minute and a much harder exam in FCC rules and regulations and principles of electronics. The testing site was at the FCC (Federal Communications Commission) field office in Columbus. Now my call sign was changed to WA8OVC. Meanwhile I found and purchased some used equipment, transmitter, and receiver, and put up some crude antenna wires.

My very first contact on my own, using code, was with a Vernon Prestwood, WA4RNG, in Chattanooga, Tennessee, on March 13, 1965. That was exciting! I still have his QSL card (confirmation postcard) in my card file. Through the years I have never lost my fascination with this wonderful hobby.[11]

Our second daughter, Tamara Jo, was born October 10, 1964, at Sheltering Arms Hospital in Athens, Ohio.

Two years later, the conference assigned us to our very own district, Delaware and Turney Center churches in central Ohio. We first lived in the town of Ostrander (Route 2, Box 196), and later moved to 109 Vaughn Road in Delaware. There we met up with Jim and Jean Ashton. I had known Jim before as a student at Mt. Vernon Academy.

One of our members at the Delaware church, Ron Smith, was an amateur pilot, and he offered me a ride in his airplane. As I was boarding, I asked about a curious shallow box of dirt under the passenger seat. He explained, "That's so I can slide it out for the people who say to me, 'You'll never get *my feet* off the ground!'"

---

[11] For more regarding my radio activities, go to https://www.qrz.com/db/kw8t.

Also, during this period I was officially ordained to the ministry at Ohio camp meeting, on June 21, 1968. Conference president Phil Follett appears at the left, and Pastor Frank Gifford at the right.

We enjoyed four wonderful years with the dear folks of Delaware and Turney Center. I even had my own radio program going during part of that time. Jim Ashton, W8FNW, and I always had a lot of fun together "playing radio," including one evening when our family was at their house and he invited me to the basement to assist him in assembling a Heathkit transceiver. We stayed downstairs well past the hour, and when we went back upstairs everyone was sacked out asleep!

Our third daughter, Michele Marie, was born on November 4, 1966, at the hospital in Delaware, Ohio. Our tribe was on the increase!

I learned that the golf course in Marion, Ohio, owned by the famous Scott Seed Company, allowed ministers to play for free on Mondays, because that was groundskeeping day. Naturally, several of us pastors took them up on the offer, and many of us in the area found ourselves there on Mondays. As you can imagine, the grounds were impeccably beautiful.

We happened to be in Memphis, Tennessee, in early April of 1968, visiting our friends Chuck and Saundra Fryling. They drove us to the motel where Dr. Martin Luther King Jr. had just been assassinated on April 4. It was not yet a memorial or anything like that, just a second-story room roped off with police tape. We stood there, mute, thinking about the tragedy that had recently occurred. It was a solemn moment, and in our thoughts, we paid tribute to one whom we now consider to be a great hero of our nation, a victim of prevailing racism.

In 1969, we attended the World Youth Congress in Zurich, Switzerland. A few weeks before we left, I happened to have a random radio contact with a Swiss ham operator, Kurt Bindschedler, HB9MX, of Winterthur, just north of Zurich. He invited us to visit him and stay a night, so we did! We went there by train. He took us all around to see the town and the beautiful Rheinfall, the waterfall on the Rhine River, and we enjoyed getting acquainted with him and his wife. He has since passed away.

We were to fly out of Dulles airport on July 20, but it coincided with the first moon landing. All airport activity stopped, as all passengers and personnel were intent on the television monitors. After Neil Armstrong stepped onto the moon's surface and uttered those famous words, "That's one small step for a man, one giant leap for mankind," service resumed, and we were soon off to Europe. The congress was attended by thousands of Adventist young people from all over the world. It was my first trip overseas, and I loved every minute of it. Vera's sister Olga and her then-husband, Allen Judefind, K3OAH, were also at the congress. There were over 50 of us representing the Columbia Union Conference, led by Ed Peterson, K3LJP, conference youth director.

Sleeping was rudimentary dormitory-style all through the meetings—guys in one building, gals in another. I became acquainted with a young man from the Philadelphia area who slept near me, John Street. Many years later John was elected mayor of Philadelphia, 2000-2008.

At one point, Vera and Olga took leave for a few days to fly to Novi Sad, Serbia, to visit Vera's birthplace and relatives of their mother. The 10-day dream trip was soon over, and we were back home.

At this time, I was the baritone for the Ohio Conference Quartet, with Roger McNeily, Roy Lemon, and Wayne Judd. I would drive to Mt. Vernon each week for our rehearsals, and we had the privilege of singing for camp meeting and in several churches.

On February 1, 1970, we moved into the new district parsonage at 295 Hickory Lane, in Delaware. But it wouldn't last long....

MISSION LIFE IN URUGUAY

One day our friend Ed Peterson, K3LJP ("K 3 Love, Joy, and Peace"), an avid ham operator, came by and said, "Jim and Vera, do you *really* want to go to the mission field?" We had applied for mission service a couple of times, filling out all the General Conference paperwork, but nothing had ever come of it. Thanks to him, in a few weeks we got word of a call to the South American Division, headquartered in Montevideo, Uruguay. We were thrilled! This is what we had been wanting to do. But now we were faced with selling our possessions, packing and crating up household items that we felt we needed as well as clothing and personal goods, selling our car, etc. It was a huge undertaking. We already had passports from our trip to Switzerland, but we would need resident visas in Uruguay and passports for the children. Just in time, an elder from our Lakewood, Ohio, church, Eugene Sheneman, bought our car.

First, though, the General Conference sent us to Pacific Union College in California for a nine-week crash course in Spanish—five hours of classes every day, each under a different professor, plus one hour of audio lab, swimming in the college pool with our fellow students and the professors, not being permitted to speak any English there, and attending the Spanish church on Sabbath. It was nine weeks of total immersion in our new tongue. Vera already spoke fluent Hungarian and a lot of Serbian and learned very quickly. I had always scored high in my Greek and Hebrew studies, so another language was not a problem for me either.

During our nine weeks there we visited "Elmshaven," the California home of Ellen White, one of our Adventist founders; San Francisco with its cable cars and lots of hippies; and the awesome redwood trees. Soon it was time to return to Ohio, pack up and/or sell our belongings, and say goodbye to our families and friends. We wouldn't see them for about three years.

We arrived at Montevideo's Carrasco airport with *many* suitcases, perhaps a dozen or so. The customs officers eyed us very carefully.

One of the "suitcases" was Vera's precious Singer sewing machine. We knew that it would take many months to receive our household goods, so we brought it with us. Not yet speaking fluent Spanish was a bit of a problem. We surely did not want to pay some exorbitant import duty. Anyway, it was a used machine. After showing the officers the matching outfits she had made for our girls and trying to explain that we were planning to reside there, they finally relented and let us through.

After a very few months in Uruguay we were both speaking Spanish quite well. In addition, our girls, after complaining the first few days that they couldn't play with the other children because they couldn't understand, picked up and absorbed Spanish in a short time and were soon speaking like natives. Ahh, kids! They did very well in church school too, sometimes surpassing the other children in language skills. They soon were involved in all the activities and became very fluent. I remember that two of their teachers were Blanca Ramos and Yoselem Testa. All children were required to wear a uniform. Good idea!

My responsibilities in Uruguay were with youth, temperance, and education. The current administration, led by President Humberto Cairus, was supportive and understanding.

Uruguay at the time was going through serious political problems. Cuba was exporting its communist philosophies all over South America. The rebels in Uruguay were called the Tupamaros. Our very first night in our temporary quarters we heard a loud political demonstration on the street outside, with threatening-sounding announcements from the passing parade—which we couldn't at all understand since we were so new to Spanish. Scary! In some respects, it was a dangerous time, and the currency became very unstable, but God was with us and protected us throughout. We even had a phone call from the U.S. embassy, as did all other Americans, warning that we needed to be extremely careful. One of the money-raising tactics of these groups was to kidnap important people and hold them for ransom.

A happy "coincidence" was that Vera had distant Hungarian/Serbian relatives in Montevideo whom she had never met, principally her mother's half-brother and a cousin and her family. We had many wonderful times getting to know each other. Around 1971 Vera's mother, Maria Poguljsky (pictured here), flew down from the Washington area to visit her half-brother, whom she had not seen since the early 1940s. The reunion was amazing! Also, we took her on a camping trip to a beautiful park near the town of Chuy, close to the Brazilian border. She stayed with us for about six weeks.

She is shown here in front of a famous monument in Montevideo, La Carreta (the wagon), honoring the original European settlers (who, sadly, drove out the natives).

Cars were old and extremely expensive. We finally acquired a 1951 Austin for about $2,000.00. It seemed that it was in the shop for repairs more often than it was on the road. It took us once on a long trip to the interior. We were all quite hungry and stopped at a town and found a restaurant. Well, I guess you could call it that. They were roasting something on a spit at this place, so I inquired  what it was. An armadillo! In this country, where the diet was mostly meat and the people ate almost anything, it was hard to be a vegetarian. Uruguay and Argentina have huge cattle and sheep ranches and have subsisted for years on their exports of meat. Where we lived, in the capital city, fresh produce was readily found, so we got along fairly well.

In a letter to my parents around Christmas time, 1970, I described sights and sounds around Montevideo:

It is summer in this part of the world. The skies overhead are a beautiful blue, the birds are singing, the palm trees wave. Occasionally a horse-drawn milk wagon rolls by, or a broom vendor calls out his wares. Scissors sharpeners ride bikes up and down the streets tooting a sort of mouth organ. Model Ts drive side by side with VWs and Chevrolets. Policemen direct traffic at major intersections, for only the downtown area uses traffic lights.

Walk down the street with us. We notice the typical Spanish architecture—houses built up against each other, concrete and stucco, balconies, bars on the windows, stone walls, patios and courtyards overhung with grapevines, red tile roofs. A little boy is kicking a ball, mimicking his favorite soccer hero. He stares at our children's blonde hair, so unusual here.

Or come with us in our 1951 Austin as we drive through the country [Uruguay is about a third larger than Ohio]. See the gauchos driving their herds and flocks. View the rolling hills, tall cacti, grassy plains, wild parrots and other birds. Notice the abundance of wildflowers and the ostriches [rheas] running wild and free.

The girls are enjoying attending our Seventh-day Adventist parochial school—all in Spanish of course. We feel they are doing quite well in picking up the language for the short time we have been here. Tammy and Mickey each celebrated birthdays since our arrival—our first "special days" away from the homeland.

Vera is getting used to a whole new system of food preparation, of course. Canned foods are very expensive and frozen foods don't exist. Fruits and vegetables are in abundance, and the kinds you get depend on the season. All meals are prepared from scratch. Certain days of the week they have the "ferias" [outdoor markets] where perhaps a hundred or so merchants will line up and down both sides of a street for several blocks to vend fruits, vegetables, cheeses, etc.

The Uruguayan/Argentinian culture included another unfortunate element—*mate* (pronounced "MAH-tay"). *Mate* is an herb, very addictive. It was common (probably still is) for men, to carry around a thermos bottle of *mate* all through the day and keep sipping away. Lunch was followed by a siesta and then a large evening meal, very late. Probably every culture in the world has something or other not so healthful—yes, even ours.

Other things we endured in Uruguay were long lines to buy needed items, such as kerosene for our space heaters (no central heating in a climate like northern Florida), milk, cheese, bottled gas, and severe fluctuations in the value of the currency compared to the dollar. If you needed something, you should have bought it yesterday, because today you can't afford it and tomorrow you won't be able to even think about it.

On the positive side, both in Uruguay and Brazil we found the young people in our churches to be so wonderful and uninhibited. They didn't become "turned off" or rude. They freely played with the younger ones and enjoyed simple games at social events. They were also very missionary-minded, looking to share their faith with others. The older folks were great too, of course.

Just before Christmas we moved into our "permanent" residence at Avenida Bolivia 2125. We were blessed with several fruit trees in the long narrow backyard—figs, pears, apples, oranges, lemons, and loads of grapevines. Our household goods finally arrived on December 22, but when we opened the crates and barrels, much of it had been pilfered in transit.

In a letter to my mother about that time, Vera wrote:

We were happy for [our barrels and crates] but we sure lost a lot to thievery. Our barrels were half empty and there were things missing from our crates even though they didn't look like they had been opened. We lost almost all our sheets, the girls' bedspreads, half our towels, half of our dishes, one whole set and parts of both other sets. Out of 24 plates we have six left, and two other odd plates which gives us eight. They stole my good set of stainless, all my sharp knives, and all my cooking utensils except for two wooden spoons. Our wedding plate was broken into crumbs because it had been unwrapped and left loose in the barrel. We're missing clothing, tools, toys, even foods, fabrics, mounting brackets for our bed, all the vacuum cleaner attachments, Corningware, just something of everything.

Ouch!

In January I was privileged to be part of a union-wide youth camping experience in Bariloche, in the Andes mountains near the border of Chile, part of the Patagonia region. We endured a 28-hour ride by bus from Buenos Aires, but it was worth it. It was stunningly beautiful, and most of the youth were seeing snow for the first time in their lives.

Shortly after that we hired a man to clean our well, which looked like it had not been used for years. We wanted the water, not to drink, but to irrigate our garden. Apparently, he didn't know what he was doing, because he climbed down into the well and then panicked and loudly cried for help, because the walls were slimy and slippery. Vera and I together could not

pull him up, so she went out front to see if she could find some help. Finally, a couple of passersby came, and we got him out. Whew!

Our son, Richard Allen, 6 pounds, 8½ ounces, arrived on August 11, 1972, born in Montevideo. Finally, after three girls! Effectively, little Ricky had four mothers! They all loved and doted on their little brother. We registered him for U.S. citizenship at the American Embassy.

I well remember a nice baptismal service I conducted in a river near the town of Melo. The local pastor was Severo Flores. The baptism took place in a lovely small river in the country. The candidate was a little lady, a midget. Just as I raised her up from the water a beautiful white heron flew overhead. It reminded me so much of Jesus' baptism in the Jordan River, when the dove alighted upon Him.

A few notable ham radio experiences took place during that time. My Uruguayan call sign was CX5AH. All through most of my life I dealt with occasional migraine headaches. I suffered most of one particular day in bed. Finally, in the evening I felt better but couldn't get to sleep. I went to the next room where my radio equipment was and began to listen around on the 20-meter band with my headphones on, so as not to disturb the family. By and by I picked up a conversation between two individuals. After listening a while, I discovered that one was in Oregon and the other on the island of Guam. And here I am in Uruguay, thousands of miles away. (Short wave can sometimes be amazing!) I listened a bit longer, and one of them happened to mention the Sabbath School lesson. Wow! These guys were Adventists! I could hold my peace no longer. I broke in and identified myself. Then, on top of all that, I discovered that the one on Guam was a dentist whose wife had been an academy classmate of Vera's! Yes, I did, I woke up Vera at about 3:30 in the morning so she could talk to her friend.

Another time I picked up a German ham operator in the city of Munich. At that time, my Uncle Bert Koeblitz was a radio engineer for the Voice of America in Munich. I told the ham my uncle's name, and he exclaimed, "Why, that's my next-door neighbor!"

Back in the States many years later, I talked to a ham in Montevideo, Uruguay. I asked him what part of town he lived in, and he said Carrasco. I told him we had lived in Carrasco, on Avenida Bolivia. Then he said he lived on Avenida Bolivia. Then I told him our house number there, which was 2125. Would you believe, he was living in the exact same house! I'm pretty sure I had left my radio tower at that house. When we returned for our mission trip in 2004, we stopped at that house, which was then a beauty salon.

Barbie's teaching ability became apparent quite early. Here we see her, on her own initiative, conducting a branch Sabbath School in our garage.

After two and a half years in Uruguay, a new "pharaoh who knew not Joseph" took over the presidency from Pastor Cairus, as he had retired. I will not give any names here, but he was one of those fellows who think they must clean house and install their own people. He was very nationalistic and resented having Americans on the staff. So, I was one of those who had to go. That was the first of two bitter experiences that we endured in our ministry. Obviously, we were quite perplexed at the time. But the Lord had something better for us. He always does!

We were then to be transferred to the state of Santa Catarina in southern Brazil, a journey up the Atlantic coast, with a new language and culture and a new phase of our lives. My departments this time were youth, Sabbath school, stewardship, and personal ministries. We took our three-month furlough in the U.S. and on the way visited our friends Paul and Coralie Cole and their children in Bolivia. We especially enjoyed Cochabamba.

Back in the States, we first took classes in Portuguese at American University in Washington, D.C. On our way back to South America we spent a delightful weekend with friends, Owen and Ann Troy, on the island of Trinidad. Friday afternoon they took us on a motorboat tour through a bird sanctuary to watch the scarlet ibis and blue herons come to roost about sundown. Tammy commented recently, "I remember this so well because there was a funeral pyre going on at the bird sanctuary while we were there. The smell is one I will never forget. That day I learned some cultures burn their dead instead of burying them in cemeteries."

My suitcase did not make it there until Sunday, which meant I had to go to church in blue jeans. When they found out that I was a pastor, they invited me to be on the platform. I was not about to do that, dressed as I was.

One thing that impressed me at church was the ladies' hats—large, gaudy, and highly decorated. I thought I was at an Easter parade! Several years later we went to a Bible performance at Sight and Sound Theater in Lancaster, Pennsylvania, and a couple of those island ladies with big hats sat down right in front of us as the show was about to begin. I complained to the usherette, and she came down and made them take their hats off. Boy, were they offended! What little hair they had was up in pins and curlers. But we wouldn't have been able to enjoy the show otherwise.

Georgetown, Guyana, followed, with a visit with Dr. Neufeld and family to see their missionary hospital. Next, we flew to Manaus, Brazil, and visited the Ronald Wearner family, captain of the Luzeiro IV, and had lunch on the launch. Or was it launch on the lunch?

Our next stop was Brasília, the ultra-modern capital of Brazil. Pastor José Maria Barboza gave us a thorough tour of this totally planned city, carved out of pure jungle. It was certainly amazing.

And here I insert one of our miracle stories:

GOD'S MIRACLE CAR

We returned to South America after a three-month furlough to begin our term of mission service in southern Brazil, in the lovely coastal town of Florianópolis. Previously we had been in the Uruguay Mission. But now we were starting over in a new place, with a new language, and unfamiliar surroundings, in the state of Santa Catarina.

All returning missionaries were to receive certain freight and baggage allowances. Eagerly we planned to use that money toward buying a car, hoping that after receiving furlough settlements we would then have the full amount required.

About 90 per cent of the cars in Brazil at that time were Volkswagens. And because we had four children, we really had our hearts set on getting a new VW station wagon, locally called the "Variant."

On our way through Brazil, before arriving in Santa Catarina, we spent a few days in the city of São Paulo, and there placed our order for the car with an Adventist dealer, expecting that by the time of delivery we would have the money. Then traveling on to our new field, we planned to return to São Paulo by bus to pick up our car.

About four weeks went by, and we still had not heard from São Paulo. We were getting a bit anxious, for they told us it would take only two weeks. We wondered what was taking so long.

Finally, the money came through from our division, also located in Montevideo about a mile from the Uruguay Mission office. We held on to this money, waiting for word to come any day about the delivery of our new car.

It is important here that I now mention several points: First, our household goods were being stored for us back in Uruguay, because our Brazilian residence papers were still being processed. We were really "camping out" in our new apartment, with everything borrowed, greatly in need of many things that were still behind in Montevideo. Also, our furlough airline tickets had been routed round trip from Montevideo to the United States and back. Since Montevideo was to our south, we had not used the return portion from Santa Catarina to Montevideo.

Meanwhile the money remained under lock and key in a desk drawer. A few days later while sitting in my office, the thought came to me, *Say, should we have returned tithe on this money? I began to wrestle*

with this thought in my mind. If we paid tithe, we would definitely not have enough money for our new car.

Being the only American missionaries there, we had no one to consult. Was this money considered subject to tithe? It was the first time we had received such benefits. Satan tempted me to dismiss the matter from my mind. But it wouldn't be dismissed. For three or four days I wrestled and asked myself how we would buy our new car.

Finally, I couldn't stand it any longer. I took the tithe amount out of the desk drawer, put it in an envelope, and turned it over to the mission treasurer. That was five minutes before noon.

I went home [a short walk across to the apartment building] and told Vera what I had done. I was very unsure how we were going to resolve the car situation. Yet strangely I felt peaceful inside, believing that I had done the right thing.

Around 5:00 p.m. that same day our office mail boy handed me a letter from Uruguay, from our friend Charles Griffin, new president of the Uruguay Mission, where I had previously served as a departmental secretary. Among other items in the letter, he asked whether I had already bought a car. If not, would I be interested in his?

Charles had previously been president of a mission in Brazil and possessed legal Brazilian residency. Before going to Uruguay, he had bought a new car in Brazil, and entered Uruguay as a tourist, hoping to continue that way, and simply drive out of Uruguay and back in again every six months or so. Automobiles were very expensive in Uruguay.

But now he decided that the arrangement was not very handy. He saw the necessity of giving up his Brazilian residency and procuring residency in Uruguay. He would have to dispose of his car. Would I be interested in a 1973 Variant with only 12,000 kilometers (less than 7,500 miles) on it?

Would I ever! We called São Paulo and cancelled our order, already way overdue (and now we knew why). We spoke with Charles by ham radio and told him we were coming down to buy the car. We obtained permission from the mission to leave for a few days, marked our already paid-for-but-previously-useless plane tickets and took off for Montevideo. We stayed in the division guest apartments and were able to see many of our old friends and Vera's relatives in Montevideo.

We went to the building where our goods were stored, seeing our precious things for the first time in four months. Then we loaded the car, inside and out, and took off for Santa Catarina, making it in about two days, about 779 miles.

Some might call all these events a series of coincidences. I believe it was God's direct leading in our lives.

Charles's letter arrived the same day I turned in the tithe, just five hours later. Buying the car was an answer to his prayers also. And we had plane tickets just waiting to be used. It also gave us the opportunity to load up the car with some of our much-needed belongings.

Was it a coincidence that by buying Charles's car the money we saved was almost three times the tithe we had turned in? "Prove me now herewith, saith the Lord of hosts," Malachi 3:10.[12]

MISSION LIFE IN SANTA CATARINA, BRAZIL

We quickly picked up Portuguese, at least enough to get along for starters, and the children soon learned it as well, since there are many similarities to Spanish.

In 1973 we attended a youth congress about 300 miles to the south, in the state of Rio Grande do Sul. The meetings were wonderful, but a real tragedy occurred the day after the meetings concluded. A bus carrying a group of Adventists from São Paulo on their way back north was struck head-on by a flatbed truck carrying a load of steel beams. The two drivers and 19 of the passengers were instantly killed, and many others were in critical condition. We went to the hospital and saw the caskets all lined up. We lost a doctor and his wife, important to our

---

[12] "The Miracle Car," published in *Insight* magazine, January 28, 1975, slightly adapted.

hospital in São Paulo. We spent the night in that same town, and the next day on the way home we saw the remains of the crash. It was very sobering.

Then, just a few months after our arrival, there was a terrible flood in late March of 1974 in the coastal city of Tubarão, a couple of hours south of Florianópolis along the Atlantic coast. This city in southern Brazil was devastated. Days and more days of torrential rains caused much destruction, inundating homes, bridges, and railroad tracks while bringing death to many. Some bodies were never recovered, having been swept out to sea. Approximately 65,000 people were left homeless. All utilities were down. All hope of recovery was seemingly dashed.

The coastal region in the southern part of our state had never had such heavy rains. Bridges were washed out, and landslides covered the roads as the rivers and streams filled up and overflowed. On Sunday, March 24, the river began to rise at an alarming rate as the rains continued to fall.

By evening the situation was getting dangerous, with some city streets impassable. People were rushing around in complete darkness, trying to save what they could.

The local Adventist pastor, Lilis Teixeira Nunes, was a real hero. Around 11:00 p.m. he began to drive all over town on roads in precarious condition to warn and rescue stranded church members and transport them to safety in the local church, which was on higher ground. Some resisted. The pastor had to go two or three times in some cases, insisting, and finally got them to the church. This took until the wee hours of the morning, even driving his VW in water three feet deep. (Our friend Lilis died November 14, 2020.)

The church was now full of children, crying for a drink of water. Finally, one of the elders began gathering water from the flood, which he strained through a cloth and boiled on a small gas stove someone had brought.

At dawn on Monday morning, they looked out of the upstairs windows on the scene. It was nothing but a sea of water covering the town, dead animals floating about, debris, furniture, etc. They were to learn later that their town of 80,000 was 95 percent affected by the flood, thousands of houses and cars destroyed, and everywhere mud, mud, mud. As the waters abated a few days later, many saw that their houses no longer existed. One church member found his house sitting on the railroad tracks. Others would find their houses still intact, but with three or four feet of mud, oozy and shiny, inside their homes, everything ruined. The newspaper claimed that over 500 had died, but a sergeant told me it was more like 5,000.

Vera and I were among those sent down to help. The local church was converted into a relief office, where typhoid vaccines were administered.

The flood was no respecter of persons. Long bread lines set up by the federal authorities stretched for blocks. Most remarkable was the fact that people of all social classes were side by side in those lines, all having been instantly reduced to poverty. Rich and poor were all now exactly equal, having a single common denominator, homeless and penniless. How fragile are the "lines" that divide the supposed social classes!

Today, more than 45 years later, Tubarão has come back. But those who lived through that experience still have many stories to tell. Undoubtedly, they learned the lesson known by all victims of tragedy—that our possessions and even our lives are fragile and subject to the whims of natural disaster, and that our first allegiance belongs to God and His work.

Our furniture and household goods wouldn't come through from Uruguay for nearly a year. Part of the problem was that it was being transported northward, and it was held up for a few weeks due to the Tubarão flood.

One Sabbath, perhaps a year or so later, I was again visiting our church in Tubarão, and was very impressed with the guitar playing of a man about my age, Roberto Alexandre. He was in a wheelchair, paraplegic. Before his conversion to the Adventist message, and before his accident, he was a professional guitarist in a dance band. Now his music was dedicated to the Lord.

I did not know it at the time, but this was the beginning of a lifelong friendship. Near the time we were preparing to depart Brazil, I encouraged him to get into ham radio so we could keep in touch. He studied hard and obtained his license a few months later, after we were already back in the States. My call sign in Brazil had been PY5ZAF. His was now PP5RL. We began to meet weekly on a certain frequency in the 15-meter band, and kept it up for many years, until the sunspot conditions changed to our disfavor. That friendship resulted in some unexpected blessings. I will pick up this story again when we get down when we were living in St. Joseph, Michigan.

I was extremely busy with my work, visiting churches all over the state, mostly by car. I vividly remember several interesting experiences:

On one of my trips out from the office, I pulled into a truck stop to get gas for my car. Going inside to pay, I stood in line behind a trucker and overheard the cashier say to him, "How much do you want me to write on your receipt?" I was very puzzled at this until I figured out what was happening. Both were conspiring in a scheme to rip off the truck driver's company. The cashier would inflate the receipt, they would probably divide up the difference, and when the driver returned to his base he would turn in the receipt for reimbursement and pocket the difference. Ouch! I was a witness to dishonesty right before my eyes. And I don't think this type of behavior is limited to Brazil.

On another occasion, I was preaching at a very rural church. During Communion that Sabbath, it was time for our traditional foot-washing ritual. My partner was an older farmer. He had never worn shoes his entire life. Traditionally, Adventists sometimes refer to this part of the service as the Ordinance of Humility. I truly "got it" on this occasion, as I stooped down to wash these hardened, calloused feet, I with two degrees after my name. I am exceedingly thankful for this humbling experience.

Another time, driving into a church member's yard in the countryside, I saw tennis shoes all along the picket fence. I asked what this was about, and I was told that on Fridays they wash their shoes to get ready for the Sabbath.

Once I was spending a weekend in the town of Joinville for meetings and staying in a hotel. Coming by the lobby, I noticed an animated discussion taking place at the front desk. It seemed that one of the guests could not access his car in the basement parking garage because it was blocked by another car. The problem? The other car had automatic transmission, which *nobody* had ever seen before (very rare at that time in Brazil) and they didn't know how to drive it! I stepped forward, borrowed the keys, and easily moved the car. Nowadays, of course, automatic cars are common there.

In January of 1974 we had a car accident while on vacation, driving our VW down to Uruguay. On the last leg of the trip to Montevideo, only 28 miles to go, with Vera driving, a car came toward us while passing another and forced us off the highway. We were near the ocean, and the berm was nothing but soft sand. She swerved to the right, went zigzagging down the road, the right wheels caught in the sand, and the car turned completely over. The windshield popped out intact and the roof caved in. The kids were in the back seat, except for Ricky, who was on my lap. Vera was trapped while the rest of us got out, bruised but otherwise unharmed. Some men pried her out. It was a miracle that we even lived through it. A couple of days later some men from the South American Division office pushed up the roof enough to get the windshield back in. We were able to drive back to Florianópolis like that. The repairs cost us $600 in 1974 figures.

In 1975 I traded our car in for a new VW Passat. Once I was supposed to conduct a baptism in a farm pond near the town of Lages. The trip took us about two hours, navigating heavy rain and muddy roads. Just before arriving the car had a flat tire. When I got out to change it, I discovered why it was flat. Someone somewhere along the line had stolen my tire and replaced it with a badly worn-out one, worn clear through to the inner tube and bald all around. It couldn't have been my tire because the car was quite new.

When the pastor and I finally arrived at the entrance to the ranch, we tried to drive in but couldn't make it up the muddy hill. We had to park the car right there and leave it, and walk three miles through mud and rain, and I in my best suit and shoes. Then I asked one of the men to indicate where I would find a restroom, and he pointed to the woods.

It was a very chilly day, with rain and occasional lightning (yes, in the mountains of southern Brazil). I entered the pond with my socks on, imagining that they would keep my feet warm. The bottom of the pond was rocks and mud. As I baptized one after another of the nine candidates, my feet sank farther into the gooey bottom until the water was up to my chest. By the time I walked out onto dry land, I couldn't feel my feet at all, and one sock had been sucked off. I pulled off the other sock and threw it in the pond too. That was Sears and Roebucks' contribution to Despraiado, Brazil. Fortunately, I suffered no damage.

On another trip I came across a serious accident. Two cars had collided head-on on the brow of a hill. One man was bleeding a lot. I helped him into my car and sped to the nearest hospital, perhaps an hour away. I later learned that he died there. And of course, there was a big cleanup job to do on my car.

Our wonderful mission president, Alberto Ribeiro de Souza, traveled extensively, as did we all in the mission office, and during the first few months he and I traveled a lot together so I could be introduced to the new places. He also helped me refine my Portuguese.

Pastor Alberto loved honey. On one of his trips he bought a square tin of honey containing about 20 kilos (45 pounds) of it. I happened to be in the garage under our apartments when he arrived. He gleefully and proudly told me about his purchase. To his utter dismay, when he opened his trunk to show me the honey, we saw it all right—all over the floor of the trunk. The tin had tipped over and opened! What a mess! He was so dismayed! (Alberto died November 13, 2020.)

Vera had the nice idea of conducting vegetarian cooking classes for the ladies of the mission. One thing she stressed was the importance of not eating between meals. Rick had just turned three, and we noticed that often at mealtime he wouldn't have much appetite. This puzzled us, but then at one of the classes a lady mentioned that Rick had knocked on her apartment door one day and begged three cookies (now that he was three, he learned that number quite well). Some of the other ladies said

that he had been to their door also. So, he had been going around to the other apartments during the day mooching food! He would go up to a door and knock, and holding up three fingers, would say something like this: "Mrs. So-and-so, I'm so hungry! May I please have three cookies [or three bananas, or three of whatever]?" No wonder he wasn't hungry! Thereafter, the expression "three cookies" (or "*tres bolachas*" in Portuguese) became a family joke.

At this point the mission voted to ask me to be the youth leader, which meant I was in charge of the youth camp on the beach at Itapema. It was quite rustic but had a nice beachfront. We often enjoyed the ocean water there. One of my innovations was to make a shuffleboard game. I painted the lines over to one side of the dining hall and made the discs and cues at home. The folks loved it, especially the pastors when they came for special meetings. I also made a ping pong table. My home church in Lakewood, Ohio, donated the money for a piano. Several years later, some wealthy investors bought this prime coastal property to build condos, and they paid the complete costs for erecting a new camp at a site a few miles away. It is called CATRE[13] (an acronym for Centro Adventista de Treinamento e Recreação) and you can look it up on the Internet. It is luxuriously beautiful, and available to tourists at certain times of the year! We know, for we visited it in 2003.

---

[13] http://catre.com.br.

We acquired a Brazilian plain parakeet (*Brotogeris tirica*). Returning home from one of my trips, I happened upon a young boy along the road selling them. I brought her home, and we named her Honey. We later learned that these boys climb trees and steal young birds from their nests, feed them a bit of rum, and then display them to sell. She cost only three dollars U.S., but when the rum wore off, she showed her naturally feisty self. That was 1974, and she lived with us for 18 years. We knew it was a female, when a few years later she laid an egg, unfertilized of course.

In 1975 the General Conference quinquennial session was held in Vienna, Austria. Afterward, a Brazilian pastor, Leo Ranzolin, who was then a General Conference official, was returning to Brazil for his furlough. Since he was originally from the city of Lages in Santa Catarina, he contacted me, as the youth director, to arrange for a region-wide youth rally at a large venue there. The meetings were wonderful and well-attended.

Are pastors' children normal? Of course, they are. Here is an insightful passage from one of Vera's letters to my parents back in Cleveland. The letter is dated October 13, 1975. Tammy had received a box of oil pastels for her birthday from Grandma.

These kids are crazy about drawing. Especially Tammy and Mickey. Ricky likes to draw too, on walls, furniture, and appliances. His and Barbie's dressers need repainting.

Here's another, from October 22: *This morning [Ricky] dumped about a quarter of a can of Nestle's Quik all over the kitchen (a big can). Friday night he glued up the furniture, piano, doors, etc. The other day he dumped soap powder all over the laundry room. And he also pulled the washer outlet hose out of the stationary tub when [I] wasn't looking, and when the washer emptied, we had a flood. (Boys will be boys, I guess.)*

On a Sunday morning in late November 1975, I drove to the city of Caçador, where I was to conduct a baptismal service that evening. I visited church members and interests in the afternoon and baptized nine people. (The minister there was not yet ordained.) About 6:00 p.m. it started to rain. Monday morning, I headed for home. Still raining, there were 70 kilometers of dirt road to negotiate before getting out to a paved highway. My breakfast that morning was only an orange and a bit of granola that Vera had sent with me. It was early and the local restaurants were not yet open for me to get a decent breakfast.

During the night it had continued raining hard and the road was in very bad shape. Things went okay until I got to a certain spot where the men had been working on the road, getting ready for paving. I almost got stuck in the mud and had to turn around and go to a different road to try to get home, but it too was in bad shape. About 9:00 a.m. the car got completely stuck. Around noon I finally found a farmer with a truck to come and pull me out. I had to walk for quite a while in my good shoes and suit to find him. Still nothing to eat. He got the car out of the mud finally about 1:00 p.m. and I drove to a little store about half a kilometer down the road. It was impossible to go on. I would have to leave the car until it stopped raining, which could have been several days. I bought some pretzels and soda pop. That was my lunch.

It looked like I might have to hole up in that place, sleeping in the car until the sun shone again. But finally, around 4:30 a car came by, heading back toward Caçador, with chains on its tires. I begged a ride and went back to town, about 60 km. We got stuck in the mud several times on the way there, but finally made it around 9:30. It was surely nice to see civilization again. I got something to eat, took a shower, and went to bed at the same hotel I had checked out of before. Oh, I also cleaned the mud off my good shoes, about three inches of it on both top and bottom.

I woke up at 5:30 a.m., dressed and went to the bus station to see if I could get back to where the car was. The rain had stopped for the moment, and I was hoping against hope to get the car out. After switching buses twice, and barely getting through the mud even with chains on the bus tires, we made it. Six and a half hours later we pulled into the town of Curitibanos and went to the pastor's house. He drove me to where I had left the car, about 30 kilometers away. I finally returned home to Florianópolis about 9:00 p.m. on Tuesday, one whole day late. Vera was plenty worried (no cell phones back then) and had even called the police to find out if there had been any accidents. Boy was I ever glad to get home! I hadn't eaten right for 48 hours, was dirty, out of clean clothes, and our new was car full of mud from top to bottom, inside and out, and slightly damaged when that truck pulled it out, with scratches in the paint and a slightly bent bumper.

DEMONS

From a letter of mine to my parents back home:

Last night I heard the devil's voice.

Most of our churches here have Sunday night meetings. Last night [at the Central Florianópolis church] when the preacher was about halfway through his sermon, a young girl stood to her feet in the audience and began to walk toward the platform, screaming. The deacons grabbed her and tried to take her out, and it was a difficult job getting her outside. Once outside, the service continued inside. At this point I happened along. I had gone to one of our other churches in town to preach and had just driven in the driveway. I saw this small group of people surrounding the screaming, writhing girl.

They took her by force down to the church school room below and began to pray and sing over her. Some of the other pastors from the mission showed up and we all began to pray over her, singing and reading from the Bible.

All the while she was screaming, in a very unnatural voice: "She's mine, you can't have her. Leave her alone. Get out of here all of you. Your Jesus is dead. I know, for I killed him." These words showed plainly that it was not just a case of mental illness.

For a bit she calmed down. By this time church was over, and we took her upstairs to her mother. But when she got inside the church it started all over again, and even worse. It took seven grown men to pin her to the floor. She was in her early 20s, I would guess. We continued singing, praying, and reading from the Bible. She continued with the same lingo. I say "she," but of course, it wasn't really she. We forced her to open her fingers and placed a Bible in one hand and The Great

Controversy *in the other. Later the Bible and* The Great Controversy *were placed on either side of her head. She tried to bite them. The church members were divided into prayer bands, in little groups all over the church. The devil was commanded to come out of her several times. It kept saying, "I won't leave, I won't leave, she's mine, I'm all alone but if you don't quit bothering me, I'll go call a legion of friends."*

Constant, earnest prayer finally won out, as about 11:00 p.m. she finally calmed down. She was able to get up and walk normally. Before she went out, we asked her to read out of the Bible, which she did, and we had prayer with her. I should add that she is not an Adventist and it was the very first time she ever had set foot in our church.

It was the first time I had ever witnessed anything like this. They tell me it is quite common in Brazil, especially up north. It was a good experience for our church members. In times like that it brings us all very much together.

Life was sometimes hard for Vera, and in a letter to my parents she confessed to times of stress and depression. I was gone almost every weekend and sometimes up to two weeks on preaching and teaching assignments, while she was left alone to raise four active children and run the household. I was glad when those days were behind us. For a time, back in Uruguay she tried home schooling as well, using the materials from Home Study Institute back in the U.S., but it proved too demanding. That's when the children began attending the local church school.

HEADING HOME?

In April of 1976, we endured a two-week nightmare of intestinal problems, skin rashes, fevers, and infections. Most of the kids in the apartment building were having the runs at the same time, so we started suspecting a common source—our water supply.

Our mission apartment building was fairly new, but because the city water pressure was low, they had constructed a large water tank on the roof. That way the water could flow in all the time, especially during the night, and being on the roof it could descend into our homes with a reasonable flow.

Since I had been on the roof before while setting up my ham antennas, I was elected to inspect the water tank. We completely drained it, and I went up to clean it. Full of mud and muck, it was overwhelming, greenish, and smelled horrible. Vera came up to help also. We scrubbed and scraped it as clean as we could get it. It seemed as if all the drains were much higher than the floor, which made it even harder. At one point when we were both tired and scraping furiously, we had a laughing fit and could hardly stop! It was really comical. We started singing the "Anvil Chorus" in rhythm with our scraping. In just a couple of days everyone was feeling better.

About this time Vera and I began to consider returning permanently to the U.S. The children were very upset about this idea, as they had made many friends in Brazil and were so well adjusted, but we wanted to put them in American schools. We wavered this way and that about when exactly to do this.

In 1976 we asked our friend Pastor João Kuntze to find us a full-size parrot. He heard of a parrot that lived on a farm near the town of Bom Retiro. It was a wine-breasted Amazon (*Amazona vinacea*) and could speak some Portuguese and German. João persuaded the farmer to sell it, then presented it to us as a farewell gift, since we were already preparing to return to the U.S. We named him Rico and had him for 37 years. We were told that he was already 60 at the time. Amazing! We brought both Honey and Rico with us to the U.S.

During our absence from the States, occasionally we would be able to do a "phone patch" to talk to our family back home. I would find a ham operator in the U.S. who had a strong signal and an apparatus that connected his radio to a telephone. Then we would ask him to dial our parents and connect us. Often in those days it would be a long-distance call for him, and we had no way to remunerate him, but usually they graciously did not expect that anyway. It was a nice service. Here is what my mother wrote after one such call:

Well, here we are, it's Friday night,
Once more I sit and try to write.
Nothing to say, nothing to tell,
Just, we're thinking about you, hope you are well.
A couple of things now cross my mind,
A call from Jim, the very best kind!
Haven't heard his voice for half a year,
When there it was, loud and clear.
Got all choked up and couldn't talk,
Was home alone, no time to balk.
So I swallowed hard and did my best.
He heard the tears, so did the rest.
That funny laugh and he said, "Poor Mom,"
While I said to myself, "They've been gone so long!"
When I hung up the phone I just sat and cried,
Let out all the feelings I'd been holding inside.
You can't possibly know until some future day
How it feels to be left when the young go away.
How I long for the day when Jesus will come
And take us all to the heavenly home,
And whenever we want, we can all get together,
And never be apart forever and ever.

Our children were dismayed at the prospect of leaving all their friends. At the time Barbie was 13, Tammy almost 12, Mickey (Michele) almost 10, and Ricky 4. They were all totally fluent in Portuguese, but of course we spoke English at home (mostly).

We applied to the South American Division for permanent return and began to prepare. We gradually sold off our furniture and other household items. We ended up sleeping on the floor on borrowed mattresses, eating at a borrowed table, and sitting on borrowed chairs. It was surprising how quickly our American-made items were taken. A young couple, Eliseo and Kátia Vidal, were interested in our clothes dryer but didn't have much money. Eliseo, a wonderful artist, offered us three of his beautiful palette brush paintings in trade, which we accepted. Pictured here is his rendition of a Brazilian village scene. It is currently in Michele and Joe's living room.

We decided to allow about a month of travel for the transition, as this was our last opportunity to do some sightseeing. We first went by bus south to Montevideo to visit family and friends, perhaps for the last time. Then on November 30, 1976, we flew to Brasília and Rio de Janeiro for a day each. We had hoped to enjoy some sightseeing in Rio, as we had never been there, but ended up going by taxi to various offices to get the export papers for our birds. No time was left to see the famous beaches or the huge statue of Christ on the mountain.

Then we flew to Lima, Peru to visit friends, and then to Cuzco to spend a day at the famous Machu Picchu Inca ruins. We all suffered altitude sickness after arriving. They treated us with a special tea—made with cocaine! Fortunately, it was a mild dose. We visited the ruins on a very rainy day, but it was still spectacular.

The birds had been left behind with our friends, but when we returned, Honey somehow had gotten out of her cage and flew up into a tree. With no small amount of coaxing, we finally got her down. Then, on to Panama City's duty-free zone to buy a new camera. The drive from the airport into Panama City to our hotel was very scary—our taxi driver was half-drunk! The next day we arrived in Miami, December 9.

Getting our birds through customs in Miami was a challenge. As we were standing in line with them in small, covered carry-ons, Honey let out a chirp. One of the officials called out, "Okay, where is that bird?" After taking us to a special room, they questioned us. Finally, they released them to us upon examining the documents and told us that they would be following up with a visit from one of their vet techs in Michigan when we arrived there. We had the Brazilian export papers to back up our story, of course. Nowadays it would be almost impossible to import a bird.

When we arrived at our hotel in Miami, Ricky asked us if we were now in America. When we answered yes, he replied, "Good, now I can speak English." He was four years old.

We were briefly and graciously hosted by the Inter-American Division of Seventh-day Adventists. Our objective was to buy a car while there, so we could drive ourselves to Michigan. We found a used Ford station wagon, thanks to some contacts provided by the Division. Then we drove up to Orlando to spend the Sabbath, enjoyed a trip to Disney World on Sunday, then on to the Washington, D.C. area to visit Vera's mother and sister, where we had a wonderful reunion. Olga and Allen had divorced earlier, and she had married Jon Yellin on October 21, 1977 about a year later. After a few days we traveled on to Cleveland to be with my side of the family.

Our final destination was Andrews University in Berrien Springs, Michigan, where I planned to apply my M.A. credits toward the new three-year degree program in Master of Divinity. We left for Andrews on New Year's Day 1977. The weather was not too bad in the Cleveland area, but the farther west we went the worse it got. We drove in a dangerous, blinding snowstorm hour after hour. The trip, which normally would take about five hours, took us perhaps 10. We finally arrived on the campus late at night, and being a holiday weekend, it was difficult to find anyone to let us into our apartment in the Maplewood complex. After knocking on a few doors, we found someone with a telephone who could help us make contact. I think they must have called the campus police, who were able to track down someone. Finally, around midnight we were inside, with our heavy suitcases and hardly any food. We were so exhausted! But it was a good thing we had unloaded the car, because by the morning the snowdrifts were higher than our front door. Talk about a warm welcome!

Next morning, we tried to walk over to the Apple Valley Market not far away, but the snow was too deep and impossible to navigate. Fortunately, a neighbor took pity on us and shared some food. A couple of days later the walks and roads were cleared, and the new semester began.

One of my favorite teachers was Dr. Mervyn Maxwell, professor of church history. Eleven years later I would become his pastor at the Benton Harbor church. He was a kind and thoughtful person.

Seminary study was wonderful, but after a couple of quarters our finances were not that great, with three children in church school. We decided to discontinue my study plan and return to pastoring. I was interviewed by Wisconsin, New Jersey, and Michigan. We decided on Michigan, and it turned out to be a wonderful, 21-year ride.

MARSHALL AND BELLEVUE

Our first assignment was in the two-church district of Marshall-Bellevue, just east of Battle Creek. The first couple of years we lived in a townhouse at 1200 Arms, Apt. 28, in Marshall. We still have a friend from those days, a Jewish neighbor, Doris DeCicco, who now lives in Colorado. We also remember that one family in that community had a cute little grey schnauzer named Oatmeal.

Eventually, the conference built us a prefab house at 1327 Verona Road, the same road as the Marshall church. We still have friends from that church. I especially remember Louise Drake, a prominent businesswoman in town, owner of the only office supply store in Marshall. She was so well known that when we went around in the fall to do Ingathering among the local businesses, they would see her coming and automatically pull out their wallets.

Among our many treasured friends from the Marshall church are Béla and Irma Krusac. Irma taught Tammy piano. We remain in touch with them to this day, although they now live in Georgia. After retiring we also lived  in Georgia and renewed our friendship. Béla and I enjoyed golfing together.

About this time, we acquired a dog, a black standard poodle. We called him Bo. I would take him with me in the mornings when I went jogging. Unfortunately, he dashed out in front of a hit-and-run driver. Bo died at the veterinarian office not long after we got him there. We were crushed. We never owned a dog after that. Now and then we had a cat, and of course we had our birds, but that was pretty much it for pets.

The other, smaller church was in the town of Bellevue. The members there were genuinely nice also. The head elder, Fred Wiesner, was a fine auto mechanic, and his wife's name was Verna. In 1981 we had an old-fashioned tent meeting across the street in the park, with Terry and Judy Wolfe and others helping.

The children were enrolled at Battle Creek Academy, which had kindergarten and all 12 grades. It was a wonderful school with dedicated teachers. Eventually, all four of our children graduated from BCA, and that may be a record for a pastor's family.

An older lady, member of the Battle Creek Tabernacle Church, had a hobby of sponsoring new area pastors to a Dale Carnegie class, so Vera and I were invited. It was great! It sharpened our public speaking abilities, and we made some new friends.

Special friends at the time were also the Eppels: Dr. Dieter Eppel, a fine osteopathic doctor; his wife, Janet; and their three children. In addition to serving as our family doctor, Dieter became our head elder for a time. He also loved sailing and kept a large sailing vessel on Lake Michigan at Saugatuck. Once he took us out sailing there. Everyone loved it, but I turned every shade of green and lost all my lunch to Neptune. This may have been related to my migraine problem, which I struggled with until my early 50s.

The Eppels left Marshall after fulfilling their five-year agreement with the Michigan Conference and returned to their beloved Finger Lakes in the state of New York. We once visited them while on vacation, at the time of the New York camp meeting. I sang a solo for one of the evening meetings, "In His Time." A night or two later a strong windstorm came through the area, tearing down the tent just as Pastor Dan Matthews stood up to speak. People had to be rescued and brought up to the girls' dorm, Dan Matthews included. I saw him many years later and mentioned it, and sure enough, he remembered.

An elderly couple in the Bellevue church was grieving for their wayward children, and often mentioned them for prayer. As time went on, the father died, then the mother, never seeing their prayers answered favorably.

Following the mother's passing I called the daughter and asked if it would be all right to visit her, and she said yes. When I entered the home, it smelled of cigarettes, and other signs of spiritual need were evident. But the visit was pleasant, and finally I asked, "Iva, have you ever considered coming back into the church?" And wonder of wonders, she replied, "Yes, pastor, I have!" Bible studies began, she started attending church, and one by one worldly habits fell by the wayside. Finally came the day of her baptism. Later Iva Barrus became the local academy principal's secretary and held that position for many years. Can you picture that joyful reunion when Jesus comes, when those blessed parents find their daughter there? Do you know anyone who needs to "come home"?

The town of Albion, Michigan, was located just a few miles to the east of Marshall. We discovered some spiritual interest in that area, so we looked around for a meeting place to rent. We began to hold services for a small number of people, perhaps 20. The town had a large black population, and several of them began attending. Not at all a problem for me, but as it turned out, I had some things to learn about their culture. At the conclusion of one of our services a black lady said to me,

"Pastor, my brother passed this week." I ignorantly replied, "That's fine, sister. What had he been studying?" "No, pastor, he died." Boy, was I embarrassed! Being a Northerner, I honestly had never heard the word "passed" used that way. We always said, "passed away." Of course, I apologized. On another occasion, a lady questioned me on the way out of church, "Pastor, when are you going to open the doors of the church?" Again, puzzled, I answered, "Sister, especially on a warm day like today the doors are always open." "No, pastor," she said. "I have been bringing my non-Adventist friend here for a few weeks. I meant to ask when you were going to make an altar call." Oops again.

NURSE VERA

During our time in the Battle Creek area, now that the children were older, Vera decided to return to college and get her nursing degree as time allowed. She started by taking some of the basic classes, such as psychology. She was already working as a nurses' aide for a home health organization. It took a few years, but we will never forget the day when we all attended her graduation service in 1983. With pride we applauded her when she walked on the platform to receive her diploma. She was now officially an R.N.! (Front row, second from the right.) After graduation she took nursing jobs at local hospitals, often involving night work. It was quite a change for our family, but we made it work. She also was into selling Tupperware for quite a while.

My Aunt Pearl in Ohio, now up in years, offered to give us her rag rug loom, a large and heavy item. She was downsizing. At that time, we had two vehicles, a Plymouth Horizon and a Plymouth Voyager with a roof rack. Naturally, we took the Voyager. After arriving in Ohio and loading the loom on top and on the inside, I quipped: "It's a good thing we brought the Voyager, because that loom's large on the Horizon." (Groan.)

Sometime during the summer of 1982, I went to the FCC field office in Detroit and passed my Amateur Extra license, requiring 20 words per minute of Morse code. My new call sign was KW8T.

MY SIBLINGS AS ADULTS

Bill (William Frank Hoffer, born June 11, 1943): I had always admired my younger brother, second son of our parents. When we were

still young and at home, we learned to play chess. He was almost impossible to beat. He could calculate moves way ahead of me. So, I pause my own story now to tell you about Bill and the others.

Bill had a passion for creative writing and was extremely brilliant at it. He began by submitting articles to a wide variety of magazines and having many accepted for publication. When he began writing books his specialty was nonfiction. He was incredibly good at researching any and every subject, even traveling to the sites of the action, such as Vesuvius. His big break came when his agent in New York called him about a potential deal. His first major book, published in 1977, was titled *Midnight Express*. It was the story of Billy Hayes, an American young man who was apprehended and jailed in Turkey for dealing in hashish. His escape from prison was daring and awesome. The book became a best seller and was even made into a movie by the same name.

In 1987 another best seller came out, also made into a movie, and later translated into many languages. *Not Without My Daughter* was the story of Betty Mahmoody and her dangerous overland escape from Iran into Turkey with her daughter, Mahtob. Through Bill we eventually came to know Betty personally. While we lived in the Battle Creek area, she was just a couple of hours north in Owosso, Michigan. We visited in her home, and she in ours, and she spoke at our church and at the academy. My personal copy is autographed by Bill, by Betty, and by actress Sally Field, who starred in the movie. I treasure it dearly.

Another winner published two years later, *Freefall*, told the story of the passenger jet that ran out of fuel at 41,000 feet over Canada. This book became a television movie and was condensed in the *Reader's Digest*. Bill was honored at Columbia Union College's 1994 alumni gathering as Alumnus of the Year.

Bill would go on to write around 20 hardcover books, many of them together with his talented wife Marilyn. Sadly, he contracted Lewy body disease and died on July 11, 2019. Marilyn had passed away earlier that year, on March 28. We miss them both dearly.

Bill's children: Jennifer Paige Hoffer Valacka and Amanda Kate Hoffer Turner, from his first wife, Edith. Amanda has become a successful freelance writer, carrying on the "author gene" of our family. Marilyn's children: Caroline Cobia Schmidt and Joseph Frank Schmidt, from her first husband, Frank.

Alice (Alice Jean Hoffer, born October 21, 1948): Alice is a professional singer and creative writer who performed with the Paul Hill  Chorale in Washington, D.C., soloed with the Robert Page Singers and Cleveland Orchestra Chorus in Cleveland, Ohio, and toured Europe with the Robert Page Festival Singers. She has also held a number of professional soloist positions at churches and synagogues in the Cleveland area and is currently the alto soloist at Rocky River United Methodist Church. Her 50-year career included writing, editing, innovation, training, creative consulting, and project management. She is also the author of a children's book, *Gretchen's World.*

On November 10, 1984, Alice married Michael Dean Sinyard, a self-taught professional illustrator for 43 years at American Greetings Corporation, and an avid bass and steelhead trout fisherman.

Together, Alice and Mike run a small group ministry in Strongsville, Ohio, and are the proud parents of Michael Joshua Sinyard, a firefighter/EMT for Tampa Fire Rescue. Josh is married to Christen (Gummoe), an elementary school teacher, and they have one teenage son, Aiden Casey Sinyard.

Dennis (Dennis Jon Hoffer, born July 11, 1954): Dennis recently retired after many successful years as a car dealership service manager. He was honored in an industry trade magazine for his exceptional service.[14] On October 12, 1991, he married Lorie Bedsole. Lorie has a daughter from a previous marriage, Nichole. Dennis and Lorie were blessed with a son, Scott Alexander, who unfortunately suffered from complications resulting from chemotherapy. He passed away on October 31, 2015, at age 23.

Dennis was the only one to follow in Dad's footsteps with a love of model building. He would sit for hours on the workbench Dad set up for him right next to his. Mom would always make him go change out of his school pants before he went to the basement because she said he hardly had any jeans without modeling glue stuck to them permanently. He still builds today, has used some of Dad's plans, and is masterful at it. He practices the art of radio control flying using some of Dad's airplanes, which he inherited.

---

[14] *PRO Sales and Service*, June 1984, p. 12.

URBANDALE

In 1984 I was called to pastor the beautiful Urbandale church, the first time in my life to pastor a one-church district. It was a nearly new building on the east side of Battle Creek, and we loved it. Also, for the first time in our lives, we purchased a house. It was from the Robert Meads, the academy principal at the time, who was leaving for another educational position. It was located practically down the road from the church at 20315 Ellen Road. The neighbors across the street didn't seem too friendly, but we got along, mostly.

Back then, conference leaders didn't encourage home ownership, since most pastors were moved around frequently. Not us—in the 35 years of pastoring in the U.S. we lived in only six locations.

The church members received us warmly. We spent much time in home visitation, giving Bible studies, preaching nearly every Sabbath, and leading out in committee meetings. It was very much a full-time job.

With no appropriate place to hold fellowship dinners though, in 1986 we launched a huge project—the building of a fellowship hall. The projected cost was $50,000, but at the time we had only $10,000 in hand. There was hesitation on the part of some, but God had a special surprise in store for us. One day the Conference Trust Services Department called and

revealed that we had just become heir to half the estate of one of our members who had passed away a few weeks prior, a very quiet old man whom we never expected to have this kind of money. Our portion would be $65,000! Added to that with mostly volunteer labor, the hall was up and functioning within a year or so. It was, and still is, a great blessing to the congregation.

The pastors of the nearby Battle Creek Tabernacle church were Elmer Malcolm and his associate Wayne Olson. Wayne had an interesting experience while out making pastoral visits. As he left one house and was going over his notes in the car, a man approached the open car window holding a gun and demanding his wallet. Pastor Olson reached for his wallet and handed it over, and the man started to leave. Suddenly the pastor said, "Wait, you forgot something." When the surprised man returned, the pastor handed him a copy of *Steps to Christ*. We will never know the result of that bold deed, at least not here on earth, and Elder Olson drove away unharmed. Whew!

While at Urbandale, we had the pleasure of uniting in marriage our oldest daughter, Barbara, to Michael Battle, on June 7, 1986. Both of them were PKs (pastor's kids), and his pastor father, Maurice, joined me in the service.

One Sabbath a lady approached me after church and told me that she felt she needed to be rebaptized. I don't take such requests lightly, so we set a time to meet privately at her home. When she explained her circumstances, I had to agree, so we set a date for the rebaptism. She was a Caribbean lady, probably around 70 years old, short, and round.

Just a week or two later, on a Sabbath morning I was down in the baptistery as the deaconess assisted her to descend the stairway. I extended my hand to help her. Now, what she had not told me was that she was wearing a wig! I said a prayer, spoke the customary words ("I now baptize you in the name of the Father, the Son, and the Holy Spirit"), and put her under the water. When she came up, she was totally bald, her black wig floating on the water, and she never even realized it! There was a collective gasp from the congregation of probably around 200 people. Trying to maintain dignity, I assisted her back up the stairs to the deaconess, picked up the wig and handed it to the deaconess, and exited out the other side of the baptistery. Back behind at the changing room, I doubled over in laughter. And I had yet to preach that morning! But do you know, not one person ever mentioned anything to me or her about it. That was the funniest moment of my entire ministerial career.

In October of 1987, the Voice of Prophecy radio ministry had a huge rally in town, with over a thousand in attendance. The following day, speaker/director Harold Richards, WD6BDZ, came by our house and used my ham radio equipment to contact his people back in California.

A physician we had met in our Dale Carnegie class invited Vera to be night charge nurse of the oncology ward of a certain hospital in Battle Creek. What she didn't know was that he had a serious drinking problem. One night a patient died, and she had to call him out of bed to come and pronounce the patient dead and then sign the paperwork. When he got off the elevator, he was so inebriated that she had to physically help him to the patient's room and guide him in signing. It was awful. Who knows how he drove home after that?

It was exceedingly challenging for her, working 11:00 to 7:00 five nights a week—difficulty sleeping and managing a household. Obviously, we all pitched in to help. But as ever she was a very empathetic and caring person, and the patients loved her. One patient in particular, who seemed at one point to be headed downhill, rallied and improved sufficiently to be able to return home. What a nasty surprise awaited her! While she was in the hospital, her greedy children, figuring that she was never going to return, had completely cleaned out her apartment, furniture and all. She opened the door and saw absolutely nothing. Naturally she was devastated. She called a taxi and returned to her hospital bed. Heartbroken and completely discouraged, she soon succumbed and was gone. Can you imagine such awful greed!

Battle Creek, for more than 100 years, has been an important part of Seventh-day Adventist history. In our early years it was the head-

quarters of the General Conference, the Review and Herald Publishing Association, the Battle Creek Tabernacle, and the Battle Creek Sanitarium, this latter location made famous by Dr. John Harvey Kellogg. His brother, William K. Kellogg, is often credited with inventing and marketing corn flakes. Pictured here is the Fieldstone Building, an annex to the Sanitarium at one time. It was demolished in 1985. Fortunately, a quick-thinking former employee, Garth "Duff" Stoltz, rescued many of Dr. Kellogg's special therapy machines, such as the mechanical horse. These items are on display at the museum on the grounds of the Tabernacle church. There is now a wonderful tourist spot, Historic Adventist Village, well worth the trip. This includes a tour of Oak Hill Cemetery, burial place of many of our "pioneers," including Ellen G. White and her family. For many years I assisted with giving the tours and possessed a key to the White's house, which is now a small museum and part of the village.

One of the personal benefits to our family of living in the Battle Creek area for nearly 13 years is that all four of our children are graduates of the local 12-grade school, Battle Creek Academy. Here we see Rick and his friends enjoying the annual Pinewood Derby.

Things went along quite well at Urbandale, I thought, until someone, an influential member (who shall remain unnamed) decided he did not like me. After about five good years at Urbandale he pulled some strings so that we would get transferred. That was my second bitter experience in the ministry, after the one in Uruguay. But *both times* God more than made up for it for me.

BENTON HARBOR AND COLOMA

I was offered the Benton Harbor church, where we remained for nine wonderful years. We sold our Urbandale house and bought a house in St. Joseph at 1509 W. Glenlord Road. Later the Coloma church was added to my responsibilities, and it was also a wonderful little church.

Ironically, Benton Harbor was the same church we had been assigned to in 1963 during our seminary experience! We were welcomed to the Benton Harbor Fairplain church by some old friends. First there was George Bush, who had been one of the deacons of the Athens, Ohio, church back in our 1964-1966 years. He was now employed in the Maintenance Department of Andrews University, in nearby Berrien Springs. He loved to tell everyone he was actually President George Bush, which he was, sort of, because he and his wife were active in the local foster parents' organization, where George was president. They adopted one of their foster children, a troubled little girl, Alice. Many years later, when we lived in the Collegedale, Tennessee, area and they lived in retirement near Nashville, we got to see them now and then. And to our surprise, that "troubled little girl' was now married!

Then there were the Maxwells, Dr. Mervyn and his wife Pauline. Mervyn came up to me and said, because he had been one of my professors years ago, "Please just be yourself and not be intimidated by having a professor in the congregation." They were always very supportive and nice. Pauline was our fine church organist.

A couple of years later Dr. and Mrs. Damsteegt and their two children, Joelle and Pieter, joined Fairplain. They became Gerard and Laurel to us. Several years later we would go with them on one of their annual Great Controversy tours to Europe. More on that later.

We were blessed to have our own church school there as well, led by principal Susan Bendrat and lower grade teacher Charlotte Anderson. There were around 50 students, including children from the other mostly black Adventist church in town. It was a wonderful mix, and we all related well.

Two young students from that era stand out. One is Dr. James Lee III, who went on to become a great music composer. A lengthy bio about him on the Internet states: "October 2006 was a defining moment in Lee's career when the National Symphony gave the world premiere of his orchestral work *Beyond Rivers of Vision* at the Kennedy Center in Washington, D.C."[15]

The second is concert pianist Alpin Hong.[16] Alpin and his younger brother, Victor, were elementary students at Battle Creek Academy during our time there. When Alpin was 12 years old their parents were tragically killed in a car accident one evening, so the boys were then raised by family members in California. We heard no more of

---

[15] www.subitomusic.com/composers/highlights/james-lee-iii/, picture submitted by Mr. Lee.
[16] www.alpinhong.com, picture submitted by Mr. Hong.

Alpin, until one day many years later I noticed a poster in a store window about a piano concert he was going to give in our area in Maryland. We informed Barbie and Tammy, and we all showed up at the concert.

We actually had front row seats. In the darkness of the theater he could not see that we were there. But at the close he was in the lobby selling and signing his CDs. We hung back until the end and then made ourselves known. As soon as he saw me, he loudly exclaimed "Pastor Hoffer!" even though he hadn't seen us in nearly 30 years. It was a wonderful reunion. Alpin's music is all over YouTube.

Our Benton Harbor Fairplain Church celebrated its one hundredth anniversary in 1990. Many former pastors and members attended, including several "missing" members. It was a wonderful success.

One of our sister churches in the Berrien Springs area, Stevensville, was planning a mission trip to the Dominican Republic. About three days before they were to leave, the organizer of the trip, a Spanish pastor in the area, called me and said that something important had come up. He was not going to be able to go as their translator, and would I consider going in his place? Of course, I agreed.

Just three days to get ready! As I was packing my suitcase and thinking about the destination, I remembered a beaten-up old baseball glove that was taking up space in a closet. Baseball is very much in the blood of Dominican boys, and a fortunate few find it to be a ticket to residence in the United States and maybe even to the Baseball Hall of Fame.

Never in our lives had we on this short-term mission trip seen such poverty! Conditions in the city were bad enough, but out in the sugar plantations were hundreds of lean-to wooden shacks row on row, often no more than three feet apart, inhabited by large families of Haitian immigrant workers, naked little children running around, chickens, flies, and filth. We were so moved by the scene that most of us ended up leaving almost all our material possessions behind when it was time to return home.

During our time there, I prayed and watched for just the right young man to appear. And sure enough, a 14-year-old caught my eye. He had been extremely helpful at the construction site every day without fail. On the last day of the project, I called him over and presented him with that baseball glove. The boy was thrilled! To him it was worth a million bucks, while for me it was just a throwaway item from the closet.

In the capital city of Santo Domingo, where we were staying, life was much better. About 15 or so of us, we had a great time working, singing, and worshipping together. We were there for only 10 days, but all of us were changed forever by what we had seen and experienced, humbled and grateful for our blessings.

And speaking of blessings! Back in St. Joseph were dear neighbors across the street. The husband worked for the Whirlpool Corporation in Benton Harbor. One of his responsibilities was to serve as chauffeur, meeting important people at the nearby airports, driving them to and from company headquarters, and coincidentally, avoiding some of the blighted areas of town, which an ordinary taxi driver might not do. As such, he was required to wear a nice business suit and tie to work every day. The Hoffers had always been faithful tithers, but at that time we were struggling financially. We also knew that God has a thousand ways to provide for His faithful children and were about to learn one of them.

One day that neighbor called Vera to say that they were planning to have a yard sale, because Whirlpool had recently changed their dress code to casual. Now her husband no longer needed his several nice business suits. Then she said something like this: "Before I offer these nice suits to the public, I wonder whether you and Jim would like to come across the street and see whether any of them fit Jim. If so, we will make a special price." Sure enough, five of the seven or eight suits were a perfect fit without any alterations. The price, $15 each! Unbelievable! And I still wear some of those suits today.

Once I was a bit late for an appointment in Berrien Springs and became frustrated on busy two-lane highway 31, right behind a slow-moving car driven by an elderly lady. After several minutes, I finally saw an opportunity to pass, so I "put my pedal to the metal" as they say and zoomed past the slow car. Pulling back to the right, I glanced in the mirror, only to discover that that "elderly lady" was Frances Dorgelo, our very own church treasurer. Oops!

Our parakeet Honey died while we were living in St. Joseph, on July 23, 1992. That morning, Ricky called out to me, "Dad, something's wrong with Honey!" I went rushing to see, and there she was, lying on her side in the bottom of her cage and trembling. She probably had had a stroke. I lovingly picked her up and talked to her, and a few moments later she breathed her last. I set her down in her cage, went down to the rec room, fell on the carpet, and bawled my eyes out. She certainly belonged to all of us, but ever since I bought her alongside highway BR-101 in Brazil, she had been my very special bird for 19 years, and I loved her. The following year I was able to publish her story in *Bird Talk* magazine.[17]

One day in 1993, my Brazilian friend Roberto, PP5RL, contacted me about a friend of his in Tubarão, Fernando Genovez, whose daughter, Milene, wanted to come to the U.S. to go to college and study English. Would we be interested in hosting her? Well, of course we would, and we began to prepare. She was going to attend Andrews University and audit various classes. Milene arrived in early fall, hardly speaking a word of English. She got along with us simply fine, and Tammy especially made a friendship with her, though there were a few years' difference in their ages. We also took her sightseeing to several

---

[17] March 1993, pages 90, 92.

places, such as Washington, D.C. But as the cold Michigan weather began to set in, and the Christmas holidays were approaching, she became quite homesick. We drove her to O'Hare airport on the 30th of December, a bitterly cold day, and she left us. A couple of years later her sister, Fernanda, came to spend some time with us as well.

In 1991 we drove Rick to Walla Walla College in the state of Washington, and then attended the SDA ham radio gathering in British Columbia. We went again the next year, and a year or two later attended the  same type of gathering at Monterey Bay Academy in California. On that trip our radiator burned up trying to cross the mountains, and we had to leave our car in a shop for several days. Some dear friends in central California, Sherman and Millie Jefferson, graciously hosted us for those few days up to the Monterey event. Meanwhile, Sherm and I battled it out in ping pong, while the ladies enjoyed each other's companionship. All this travel was in addition to attending hamfests (ham radio expos and flea markets) all over the country, sometimes two or three times a year, plus personal vacation trips to visit family and friends.

A great tragedy occurred in 1993. Two people from Battle Creek Academy joined the cult of David Koresh. One had been a student, Jeff Little, and the other was a beloved teacher, Sherrie Jewell. They both died in the Waco fire. It was such a shame, and their families were obviously devastated. How can people get mixed up in stuff like that? We must never follow a human, only God. Sherrie was Tammy's favorite teacher.

One day I received a phone call from Mary Engle, one of our church members. She sounded quite excited and wanted Vera and me to come by her house to hear a marvelous story. Her elderly mother and disabled brother had been living with Mary and her husband for several years, but the mother had recently died. Now a few days had gone by, and

Mary had visited the Social Security office to report her mother's passing. Little did she know the surprise she was about to receive.

She handed over the death certificate and was going to arrange to halt her mother's monthly benefits and change her handicapped brother's benefits to herself. Then the lady said to Mary, "What about the benefits from your father?" To which Mary replied, "My father has been dead for many years." Then with a strange look on her face the lady said, "No, dear, your father is very much alive." Mary was totally shocked! Then the lady said, "Listen, I am not allowed to reveal his whereabouts, but if you will write a letter, we will forward it to him."

As she later found out, Mary's parents had gone through a very bitter divorce when she and her brother were quite small, and her mother never spoke about her father. All she remembered was that as a very little girl, they were exiting down the front steps of a big building (which she later realized was a courthouse in Chicago) and her mother was sobbing terribly. Needless to say, a few days later Mary's dad called from Chicago after receiving her letter, and it brought about an exceedingly happy reunion! She was also able to connect with half-sisters she never even knew about. God is so good.

Michigan camp meetings were always huge and awesome, with Sabbath attendances estimated to be as much as 10,000. After 21 years in Michigan, that is one thing I greatly miss.

But I can't think of Michigan without regretting the time I missed a golden opportunity to tell a huge joke. It was at a pastoral retreat at Camp Au Sable near the northern town of Grayling, about the time of the Gulf War in the Middle East. The summer weather was hot and humid, and there were swarms of bothersome houseflies. One day our conference president, Elder Jay Gallimore, began a meeting with these words: "Folks, before we get started, does anyone have any idea of how to cope with all these flies?" This was one time I really missed it, for I should have stood up and made this statement: "Sir, I have two suggestions. First of all, you are the president here, and you can declare these grounds a 'No fly zone.'" In the context of the times, that would have brought the house down, I think. Then I would have said, "Pastor Gallimore, when I was a little boy, on vacation in Pennsylvania with my parents and my younger brother, the flies were so awful that my mother gave us each an empty mason jar and a fly swatter, and promised us a penny for each dead fly we would bring back. And boy, did we go to work! I suggest we do the same here."

One winter pastoral retreat we attended at Au Sable, we woke up one morning to -18 degrees! Ouch!

And I cannot leave that topic without recounting a humorous camp meeting story, another time, another place:

Several years ago, a certain Adventist conference had a big tent for their main meetings (and some still do). At the back was a wooden structure that served as the sound booth and the main control point for public address across the campus. In the booth was an intercom telephone connected to the various outlying departments.

A pastor friend of mine, Paul Gates, KW4BD, was on duty in the booth when a curious thing occurred. Just as someone on the platform was about to offer a prayer, the intercom phone rang. The pastor on the

platform began with "Dear Lord..." and at that precise moment Paul, back in the booth, distracted, picked up the phone and in a rather strong stage whisper said "Ye-e-e-s." Of course, everyone in the audience heard it and chuckled.

By the way, I still have my keys from the old Grand Ledge camp meeting: our cabin, our audio studio, and the main pavilion, where I assisted with the sound system. That campus is now full of houses.

MISSION TRIP—PHILIPPINES

We had the privilege of being involved in several mission trips over the years—Dominican Republic, Philippines, Yugoslavia, Brazil, Uruguay, and Cuba. In every instance we have been extremely blessed and would highly recommend that every able-bodied person try it at least once.

We found that most people responded readily to our fund-raising letters for our various expenses, but we were hardly prepared for one of the responses. As we were getting ready to go to the Philippines, for example, we opened one letter and found inside a check for $1,000! It was from my Uncle Roy Koeblitz in California, not an Adventist, who had served in the Philippines in World War II. He said in his letter that he wanted us to go and "be comfortable."

Everywhere we've gone on a mission trip, the pastors, conference personnel, and church members have received us with open arms and hearts. Not once have we had a negative experience. It has always proved to be a blessing and a time of personal growth.

In 1996 we assembled a small team of six people from our two churches and went on our three-week evangelistic tour of the Philippines. Though it was very hot constantly, it was still a blessing. We were on the southern island of Mindanao, in the town of San Francisco. We preached every night in a meeting place holding about 300 people in a village called Patin-Ay. My sermons were translated into Cebuano for those who did not speak English, although many people do. English is taught in all the schools.

Consider the experience of newly baptized and newlywed Stephen Murdock. Up to this time, he had been a factory worker with no pastoral experience. But wanting an adventure with God, he joined up with our small mission team headed for the Philippines. The other team members were his wife, Dolenda, Jason Carlson, Harry Rogers, Vera, and I.

On March 25, 1996, Jason's father drove us from Berrien Springs to O'Hare airport in Chicago in a terrible snowstorm for our overnight flight to our first connection in Seoul, Korea. Vera and I had planned a little surprise for Dolenda, since her birthday was March 26. When midnight came, we sang "Happy Birthday" to Dolenda and passed around Little Debbie cakes to everyone, but hers had an unlighted candle. After a couple of hours, the pilot announced that we had just crossed the International Date Line, which meant that her birthday was only two hours long! The nonstop flight from Los Angeles to Seoul, Korea, took 13 hours (but on the way back, only nine hours—due to the prevailing winds).

In Manila we were very concerned about going through customs, because of all our equipment for the meetings, the overhead projector especially. Providentially, Elder Jim Zachary was on our flight, the organizer of our "Target 50,000" effort, and a very experienced world traveler. He approached the customs officials and explained our mission, and they waved us right on through without opening a single piece. We got out of the airport and were transported to our place of abode, the Hyatt Regency Hotel—an expensive but welcome sight after a marathon trip of 36 hours. Add to that the fact that we had already been up several hours before we left home. Needless to say, we literally crashed when we finally got checked in to our rooms.

We arrived in Butuan the next day and were met at the airport by the president of the Northeastern Mindanao Mission, Pastor Luciano T. Nermal, a very pleasant and warm individual. He and a driver took us directly to the mission office, where we were surprised by a lovely welcome banner and the office staff waiting to greet us. School teachers from the several mission schools were there also, as school had just let out for the "summer" (how can they tell?!) and they needed to finish their yearly reports. A wonderful meal was also spread out for us, and it was so refreshing to finally get some good Adventist cooking! Then we left in the van for the two-hour drive to our next lodging in a small town called San Francisco. Nearing our destination, we stopped at Patin-Ay to see the auditorium where our meetings were to be held. Then we continued to the Laguna Lodge, which was the hotel for our entire stay. We were assigned a room near the front of the building, tiny and spartan, but at least it was air conditioned. That evening we began our regular meal schedule at the home of Elena and Nathaniel Ebarle, a wonderful Adventist couple. The meals were planned by another Adventist sister, Evelyn Pangan, widow of a former mission president who was killed in an airplane accident in 1990. We enjoyed a delicious meal, including many tropical fruits and many new flavors. We took time to practice some of our music before retiring to our rooms.

We had a good time at our meals, which were always held at the Ebarle home with several ladies attending. One day Vera recounted her experience in making cloth "she bags" for us, staying up past midnight to get them done for the trip. They would otherwise have been known as "shoe bags," but we discovered that she had gone all the way around the bags with her new embroidery machine, accidentally leaving out the O—and we split our sides laughing!

At the meetings, Stephen and Dolenda handled the nightly family life talks, Harry and Jason the children's ministries, and Vera and I the main stage.

One afternoon, the local pastor came by and announced that we were going to do some prison ministries that day. We boarded the van and rode out into the countryside to the local prison. The ladies were instructed to remain outside the gate to sing and pray. The men entered the compound. There were probably half a dozen cell blocks, filled beyond capacity with men, who in many cases had to take turns using the beds. Then the pastor said, "Jim, you are going to preach to that cell block; Jason, to this other one; and, Stephen, over there." This was done with no forewarning, and Stephen, a new believer, had never preached a day in his life! But he swallowed hard, said a quick prayer, and with Bible in hand preached to nearly 30 prisoners in that cell block. Not long after that, back in the U.S., he began to prepare for the ministry himself. Whom God calls he enables! God does not just want our money. He wants our hearts!

One afternoon I was privileged to baptize about 65 prisoners out in the courtyard in a steel drum.

April 4 was Jason's birthday, his 18th, and we arose at 4:30 a.m. to prepare for a trip to the ocean. As we were about to leave the hotel at 5:00 we heard singing coming from out in the entryway. A group of local youth from the San Francisco church came by to sing "Happy Birthday" to Jason. It was a very moving experience and brought tears to Jason's eyes. They presented him with cards and gifts. Then we loaded into Fred Kho's van and took off for Bugad Beach on the ocean, near a place called Barogo. It was a two-hour trip, about 25 miles, over a few good roads and some very bad ones. (Average speed 12.5 miles an hour!) We ate breakfast in one of several booths at a park along the beach, then went swimming in the beautiful China Sea and walking along the beach. Some picked up shells and coral. Back in town in the evening we again celebrated Jason's birthday at suppertime with a cake and more singing. Jason will remember this birthday as long as he lives! Jason became a literature evangelist back home, later a conference publishing director, and more recently a pastor. Harry, a schoolteacher, became a pastor and served for many years in the Michigan Conference. How a mission trip can change people!

I celebrated my 56th birthday on April 12. The last time I had observed my birthday on foreign soil was 1976 in Brazil, exactly 20 years earlier. On this morning we were awakened at 4:30 a.m. by a group from the Patin-Ay church serenading me. They presented me with a lovely bouquet of roses and bird-of-paradise set in palm branches, a knitted sweater, a bag of sticky rice dessert, and a poster. At breakfast I received several additional gifts and cards. It was very moving to see the generosity of these people who have practically nothing. Their churches are for the most part in poor repair or unfinished, and their homes likewise. Yet they are radiantly happy because heaven is their true home.

Harry had brought along a small suitcase full of puppets. At the meetings, Elleneth Ebarle, in her teens, showed her abilities by organizing and presenting the puppet shows. A couple of years later, Harry and his wife Ingrid returned to hold meetings on their own, then sponsored Elleneth to the U.S. to study at Andrews. She stayed in America and married Gabriel Engelkemier. They still live in Berrien Springs and have three children.

It was now our last day of meetings, Sabbath, April 14. As we arrived for breakfast at the Ebarle's home, Pastor Nermal awaited us, and we saw a large cloth covering something on the coffee table. There were four beautiful hand-carved water buffalo, one for each of our families, as a farewell gift from the mission. Once again, we were overwhelmed by the graciousness and generosity of our Philippine friends.

We proceeded to the sports complex for our worship services at the grandstand, with around 1,000 in attendance from all the churches of the district. There was no Sabbath school, as a baptism was planned. The grandstand bordered the large Olympic swimming pool on two sides. After I presented a message on the Spirit of Prophecy, the 77 baptismal candidates came forward, and four of us pastors entered the water to proceed with the baptism. It was a very moving sight and brought our total baptisms for the crusade to 195. Once those who had responded to our appeals had receive their studies and prepared, the baptisms may have reached 300.

The afternoon meeting convened at 1:30, where I presented the final message about Christian standards. Vera and I closed with a duet to end the service, but it was very hard to finish the song and closing prayer because of the falling tears. After sunset we returned, where an evening social was already in progress—a grand march, just like we used to do some 30 years ago during our academy days. It was refreshing to see young people who weren't tainted by western sophistication. As the social was about to conclude with singing by a large group from one of our schools, Pastor Retuerto and Brother Kho presented us with further gifts, hats and baskets made out of straw.

The following day we traveled to visit Mountain View College, a beautiful school in the mountains to the west. I visited with several members of the MVC ham radio club and their president, Wendell Paypa, DU9DRW (now AE6WR), and soon headed back to Manila and home. On the way we stopped at a humble Adventist clinic and left a large supply of medical items. Vera, the nurse for our team, had brought along basic supplies, and fortunately they were hardly used. The people at the clinic were extremely grateful to get them. A couple of days later we were back home in Michigan.

Vera's mother had been living with us now for quite some time, and her memory was failing considerably. One evening in March 1997, while we were out for a bit, she was looking for us and fell partway down a flight of stairs. When we drove in, there she was crumpled on the floor and hurting. We called an ambulance, and they took her to the hospital. She had a fractured collarbone and some bad bruises. From that point on she was placed in a care facility. It was a difficult decision, but it was time. Altogether she lived with us for about eight years.

Adventists generally observe Communion once a quarter, and the option of a foot washing ceremony is included. On one occasion, a new member named Alex joined our Fairplain church, and was deeply impressed with seeing Communion for the first time. He requested that we take the service to his home for his wife, severely afflicted with Alzheimer's. Sometimes in a case like this we omit the foot washing, but he had already prepared. As Vera and I sat watching, he brought out a basin, towel, and soap, and proceeded to wash her feet. This time I was the one who was deeply moved. It was evident that despite his wife's inability to reciprocate, or even understand what was going on, he dearly loved his life companion. It was amazing!

Back in 1964, when the seminary had assigned me and another student to the Benton Harbor Fairplain church, we met a wonderful couple there, Phil and Carol Hopkins. I remembered that they invited Vera and me to dinner after church one time. Now, here I was at that same church as a full-time pastor 35 years later. In the meantime, Phil had died.

A sobering tragedy occurred during my final year at Benton Harbor and Coloma. We had our church board meeting on the evening of February 9, 1998. Our treasurer, Carol Hopkins, was present and all seemed well. But a couple of days later our school principal, Susan Bendrat, needing some financial information, tried several times to call her, without success. Finally, Susan drove to Carol's house on Kephart Road in Berrien Springs. Her car was in the driveway, but she didn't respond to the doorbell. When Susan peeked into the front window, there was Carol, lying on the living room floor, apparently unconscious. Susan called her son Jim, and they went in and found her dead. She was 75, and apparently had had a heart attack. She had been dead for a couple of days.

Not only had we lost a wonderful treasurer, but she was the only one who knew the password to the church treasurer software. It took me over a week to reconstruct the records and get things caught up.

By the way, down at the end of Kephart Road was a large gate, and on the mailbox a small plaque that read "M. Ali."—the home of the retired famous boxer, Muhammad Ali. That home many years ago had belonged to Al Capone.

HAGERSTOWN, MARYLAND

Bob Kinney was president of the Review and Herald Publishing Association in Hagerstown, Maryland, for several years, and a member of the Willow Brook church there. In 1998 he attended the Mount Vernon Academy alumni weekend for his 50th class reunion and heard me present the Sabbath school lesson representing my 40th (1958) class. At the time, his church was without a pastor, and when he returned home, he recommended me to Conference President Neville Harcombe. A few days later, Neville called me out of the blue, and asked to interview me to consider a position in the Chesapeake Conference. At the time, I had been pastoring Benton Harbor/Coloma district for nine years. He asked me to meet him at Midway airport in Chicago to catch him partway on a trip back home.

I drove to Chicago, we met and talked, and I soon received an official call. But the Hagerstown church was also without a pastor, as Tim Roosenberg had just left for another assignment. Elder Harcombe gave me the opportunity to choose, and after consideration I chose Hagerstown over Willow Brook, despite the huge construction debt.

We purchased a home at 58 Byron Drive in Smithsburg, just a short drive to the east. We made many friends in the neighborhood and in the church and lived there for 12 years.

What to do, though? The church was barely meeting its monthly mortgage payment to the conference Revolving Fund, and some months not meeting it at all. Here's what happened and how the dynamics changed.

An Adventist financial consultant was contacted to help get over this hump, but he required further expenditures to get the campaign going—several thousand dollars. Would the church buy into this plan? Now, think of this from a business standpoint. Businesspeople know that you must spend money in order to make money. A brand-new business cannot make even its first dollar until there is expenditure for office space, furniture and equipment, advertising, raw materials, and such. Sometimes a church needs to think like a business.

It was important to sell the idea to the church that an expenditure of $40,000 would be needed in order to pay off the debt of nearly $800,000. So, I posed a question to the church board and later to the church in business session: "Would you spend $40 to make $800?" Of course! Proportionately, that is what would be taking place. The church voted to go ahead, and with God's blessing the debt was entirely paid off in five years. But that isn't the best part. During those five years, tithe and offerings for all the other church funds were up as well! How do you explain it? Enthusiasm for God's work!

In 1999 we pastors and our spouses joined the Chesapeake Conference leaders on an awesome trip to Israel. Here I'll share just one little vignette. When we got to Jericho, a camel driver was giving us short camel rides for a nominal sum. When I got down from the camel at the end of my ride, the grizzly-bearded driver planted a scratchy kiss on my cheek!

A singular experience occurred while pastoring in Hagerstown. One Sabbath morning a lady named Ruth Yates visited our church for the first time. After the service I approached her to get acquainted. She told me that she had been raised Adventist and graduated from Union College in Lincoln, Nebraska. However, during her young adult life she met and married Dick, not an Adventist, who was headed for a career in the military. At that point she stopped attending church. After serving for 20 years, Dick took his retirement and felt called to the ministry. Having prepared for that, he served in several places and accepted a position in the Hagerstown area. But God was tugging at Ruth's heart to return to the church of her childhood. Needless to say, Dick hit the ceiling. Imagine the pastor's wife being of another denomination! But she stuck to her decision, and so made her appearance at Hagerstown Seventh-day Adventist Church that day.

I called at their home one afternoon, and Dick came to the door. He gruffly let me in to talk with her but wanted no part of it. Soon after, Ruth was rebaptized and joined our church. A year or two passed. Occasionally Dick would attend our church with her, but then he would hear something in my sermon that he strongly disagreed with and did not mind telling me so on the way out. In fact, he even once said that he was never coming back.

Then it was time for a series of satellite evangelistic meetings featuring Doug Batchelor. Several members of our church had assignments to help with the meetings; hers was to sort and prepare the handouts for the night. He came along to help her with that. And then, as the evening presentation was about to begin, they would sit together on the very back pew, as far away as possible.

Very gradually Dick's whole attitude began to change. Of course, who isn't intrigued with Doug Batchelor's sermons? By the end of the series he was a different man, and I baptized him into our fellowship. By this time, he had retired from his last church pastorate.

That was the first time ever for me to baptize a minister of another denomination. We're still friends to this day.

On April 29, 2001, we acquired a new bird, Pepper, a Mexican yellow-nape parrot (*Amazona auropalliata*), actually a rescue bird that Tammy found for us.

Another interesting thing happened while I was pastoring the Hagerstown church. One day when I was working in my church office, someone came to the door. It was a representative of one of the prominent cellular services. He wanted to know, since our church had a nice carillon tower, and was located at one of the highest points in town, whether we would allow them to install a cellular repeater there. Well, we got approval from our church board and the Chesapeake Conference, and to this day that cell tower is still in service, bringing in additional revenue to the church.

We have always been a fun-loving family. One of our simple games was "Pull Daddy off the sofa," and later, of course, "Pull Grandpa off the sofa." Of course, Dad/Grandpa was also always good for piggy-back rides.

TRAVEL, VACATIONS, AND MISSION TRIPS

Here is a summary of my travels, most of the time with Vera:

1969 – Our visit to the World Youth Congress in Zurich, Switzerland.

1970 – Our move to Montevideo, Uruguay, and several trips throughout Argentina and Paraguay.

1973 – We visit friends and do sight-seeing to and from our furlough, in Bolivia, Ecuador (airport only), Panama, Guyana, and Trinidad.

1974 – We drive to Iguaçu Falls, then cross over into Paraguay, and return to Santa Catarina via a ferry boat.

1976 – We visit Peru on our final journey home, spending a day at the Inca ruins of Machu Picchu (very rainy that day).

1991 – Dominican Republic (previously described), trip to British Columbia and Alberta.

1996 – Korea (airport only), Philippines (previously described).

1999 – Israel, a fantastic pastors' tour sponsored by the Chesapeake Conference. There is nothing like following in the footsteps of Jesus and the Apostles.

2002 – Germany, Serbia, Romania.

2003 – Mission trip to Tubarão, Santa Catarina, to conduct a series of evangelistic meetings.

2004 – Mission trip to Montevideo, Uruguay, with a team of helpers from the Urbandale church, to refurbish a neglected community services center there (October 10-22).

2006 – Reformation Tour to Germany, with Pastor Don Schneider.

2007 – Music tour to Germany, Austria, and Czech Republic, with Shenandoah Valley Academy.

2010 – Great Controversy tour to Italy, Vatican City, Switzerland, Germany, France, led by the Damsteegts.

2017 – Cuba, evangelistic meetings.

2019 –Uberlândia and Tubarão, Brazil, to teach my Lost Ark Seminar series.

In addition, as world president of the Adventist Amateur Radio Association International 1990-2020, we traveled extensively throughout the U.S. and Canada. I represented the AARAI at a booth at General Conference sessions in Dallas (1980), New Orleans (1985), Indianapolis (1990), Toronto (2000), St. Louis (2005), Atlanta (2010), and San Antonio (2015); and taught amateur radio at Oshkosh Pathfinder Camporees in 1999, 2004, 2009, 2014, and 2019. My dear friend, Erwin Bishop, WB7ATT, since deceased, was a great help in our booth (below).

We loved to go to General Conference sessions! Being longtime church workers, we knew and would meet literally hundreds of old friends, many of whom would also be there for the 10-day series.  A particularly memorable experience occurred at the session in St. Louis in 2005. The subway station was located just outside the main hall. After one evening's meeting the platforms on either side of the tracks were crammed with thousands of people heading for their hotels. The guard on our side, the only guard there, seemed particularly nervous because there was no railing or barrier of any kind between us and the tracks below. Any slight surge of the crowd could have resulted in someone falling. So, Vera and I started singing a song that is well known by Adventists and exists in many languages, "We Have This Hope." Immediately those around us picked up on the song too. In moments, the whole cavernous place was ringing with thousands of singing voices. The crowd relaxed, and so did the guard. It was a wonderful and memorable moment.

We have had some unusual experiences on our vacations, like the time we went to see Old Faithful at Yellowstone. On a cold, drizzly day there were few visitors. But near us were two young boys from two different families. They introduced themselves to each other and told where they were from. When one said he was from Michigan, we asked him where in Michigan. He replied, "Well, you probably wouldn't know, because it's a small town." "But," I said, "tell us anyway." So, he said, "It's near a town called Berrien Springs." Which we knew very well, because of Andrews University. So, he further explained, "Actually, it's Stevensville," very near where we had lived. As a matter of fact, his house was almost around the corner from our house—and we had traveled over a thousand miles to meet him! Another time we saw a pastor friend of ours at the famous Wall Drugs, a popular attraction along Interstate 90 in South Dakota.

In retirement, my father was an excellent gardener. He took great pride in his home-grown tomatoes and cucumbers as well as other things. In the fall he would do a lot of canning, including making dill pickles. Pictured is a birthday card they sent me, inside of which Mom wrote the following: "I don't know if you ever saw one of these cards or not, but these are some of your father's tomatoes. It was probably 1994 or 1995, and the photographers at American Greetings asked Alice [my sister, who worked there many years as a writer] to bring in some of his tomatoes to photograph. I was surprised when I saw this one in the store and thought you would get a kick out of it." On the inside it says "… different from all the rest!"

My father was always full of puns and jokes, even at the last. Now you see where I got it! Anyway, at 84 he was diagnosed with colon cancer. As they were wheeling him into surgery, he looked at us and said, "Well, they are going to change my colon into a semicolon!" Unfortunately, he died a few days later in the hospital, May 21, 2000. It was his last joke.

GERMANY AND SERBIA

Early in 2002 our friend Pastor Nick Satelmajer invited us to go to the former Yugoslavia[18] to hold a series of evangelistic meetings for five weeks in the brand-new Adventist church in the city of Novi Sad, Serbia. We immediately accepted, since Novi Sad was where Vera was born in 1942, and she still had relatives there. We wrote our typical fund-raising letters, and many helped us realize this dream. We also took a class in German at Hagerstown Community College, free to senior citizens, that was extremely helpful for this trip (and other trips we didn't yet know about).

On the way, we visited a German ham radio friend, Max Nagel, DL9KAB, with whom we became acquainted while living in Brazil. He was now living in Bonn with his wife, Lore. We had a wonderful time together.

After our overnight plane trip on April 8, followed by the train ride from the Cologne airport to Bonn, we were jet-lagged and very tired. But Max insisted that we not rest at all. He planned to take us around town to see the various attractions and keep us awake until *their* bedtime. One special place we enjoyed was the home of Beethoven. (Yes, he is still decomposing!) You know, it turned out to be the absolute best for us. We awoke the next morning fresh and ready to go.

He drove us on the autobahn and got up to over 100 mph! We visited Cologne, including statues of the city mascots Tünnes and Schäl, two figures from Hänneschen-Theater, the puppet theater of Cologne; the massive cathedral; the Kölner Dom; and many other sites. One more night of rest and it was off to Belgrade and then on to Novi Sad about an hour north.

---

[18] Prior to the Balkan War, the various states had been artificially combined into the country of Yugoslavia. Our meetings were held in Serbia.

Varadinski most
01.04.99. 05:05

Sadly, Novi Sad (translation "new plantation") still bore the marks of the 1999 Balkan war. Some of the main bridges across the Danube had been destroyed by bombings. The people of the area were astounded and very angry that their city had been bombed. They had not been involved at all in the war. On the back of this postcard is written, sarcastically, "Greetings from Novi Sad, where the Danube flows *above* the bridges."

The evangelistic meetings went very well. We enjoyed the people immensely, and we did spend time with some of Vera's cousins, aunts, and an uncle. Her mother, Maria, had been raised in Novi Sad. She was really more of Hungarian extraction, while Vera's father was Russian. One day we walked by the Hungarian Reformed Church, where baby Maria, and many years later, baby Vera, were christened. We happened to find the pastor there in his office. He showed us around and then went to a file cabinet and pulled out the membership records. Sure enough, Maria's name was there, as well as Vera's. So, the pastor made out a membership certificate for Vera, calling her a "member in good standing."

Now here's something that happened in connection with the meetings themselves. During that time, we were assigned to have lunch each day in the home of one of the church families. On April 16, we found ourselves in the home of Lazar and Jasmina (Lazarus and Jasmine, in English). Seated at the table, we heard one of the most wonderful stories of God's providence.

Lazar and Jasmina had been avid and loyal Communists during the Tito regime. However, they began to notice that some of the party officials had nicer homes and cars, and soon disillusionment set in. (You've heard the old saying, in Communism everyone is equal, but some are more equal than others.) One day Jasmina accepted the invitation of an Adventist friend to visit our church there. She very much liked what she heard, but Lazar was not interested. Sometime later, evangelistic meetings were in progress and Jasmina tried to get Lazar to attend. After days of urging, he finally consented, but wasn't interested in the presentation. In that darkened auditorium, he decided to take a little nap instead.

The message that evening was on the subject of death and the resurrection. During the story of the raising of Lazarus the pastor called out, "Lazar, come forth!" (John 11:43) Lazar shot up in his seat, turned to his wife and said, "How does that man know my name?!" Now, of course, he was wide awake! He began to listen intently to the message, and, well, you guessed it—a few weeks later Lazar was baptized into the Novi Sad church.

VERA'S FAMILY HERITAGE

This seems a good place to interject some family history. Vera's mother, Maria Keri, was the firstborn of a loving and religious family of the Hungarian Reformed Church, a Calvinist, earn-your-salvation, religion. Her parents were Hungarians who because of political disputes over territory lived in what was then Yugoslavia. When she was just two years old her mother died in childbirth. Soon thereafter her father remarried, and more children were born to the couple.

Near the beginning of World War I, Maria's father was killed when she was only seven. She was no longer wanted. After having been beaten unconscious by her step-mother, she was rescued by an aunt and uncle from her mother's side of the family. She became the youngest by 10 years of a family of five children. Now she was well cared for, but there were still problems. While all her cousins married, she was expected to stay single to care for her adoptive parents in their old age.

Vera's father, Aleksei Poguljsky, was born in Saratov, Russia, in 1899. He had fought in the Bolshevik Revolution in Russia, and when his side lost, he had to flee for his life. His family stayed behind even though they had lost land, title, and possessions to the Communists. They had been dispossessed of their beautiful mill and farm, as it was now being "nationalized." He fled west to Serbia, where the language was somewhat similar, and resettled. There he met and married Maria, though she was 10 years younger than he, on February 10, 1940.

Vera was born in Novi Sad, on May 29, 1942. When she was just over two, her mother had to flee Yugoslavia because of her father's affiliation with Hitler. They were able to hitch a ride with neighbors who had a horse and cart and traveled across Yugoslavia west to Italy. Because of heavy snows they wintered in the woods under a huge evergreen in the Italian Alps. By this time, her mother was very pregnant. Somehow, they made it to Czechoslovakia, where Vera's sister, Olga, was born in a German field hospital, on February 2, 1945, near the town of Weipersdorf.

Yes, believe it or not, her father had joined up with Hitler's army! Why would he do that? Because Hitler had sworn to conquer Russia and the Bolsheviks and return everyone to their homes and livelihoods. I have in my library a remarkably interesting book titled *Russian Volunteers in Hitler's Army 1941-1945*, published in 1997 and written by Lt. Gen. Wladyslaw Anders, which gives the whole story. It is not well known. Anyway, Aleksei was captured by the British, and in a prisoner-of-war trade was sent back to Russia to serve in one of the slave labor camps of Siberia. He died in 1956. He had refused to use forged documents that could have gotten him out of prison.

Maria and the children spent about four years in several different refugee camps in Austria. At this point Maria had given up on religion. If God existed, why did He permit so much suffering and loss? A loving God? Impossible! She didn't want anything to do with Him. Through all her years in Europe she continued attending her Reformed Church, until...

Another Hungarian woman in the camp befriended her. Antonia was quite a bit older than Maria. She tried to help Maria in any way she could, including encouraging her to study the Bible. She was kind, helpful, and caring. At first Antonia would just talk about her loving Creator and how He cared about His creatures and even victims of war. She told Maria the story of Satan and the reason there was so much sorrow in the world and gave her a Bible.

Slowly Maria's concept of God changed. She diligently searched her Bible for answers. For weeks on end she studied without telling Antonia. Then one day there was a discussion about the seventh-day Sabbath along with Bible proof texts. Still she gave no clue to Antonia about the struggle in her heart. When Antonia left, she read and reread the texts several times. She was beginning to really see God's loving plan.

Two days later, Friday found Maria cleaning up their little room in the barracks. She was on her hands and knees scrubbing the floor when Antonia stopped by. "See what I'm doing?" she asked.

"Sure, you're scrubbing the floor," answered Antonia.

"But do you know why I'm doing it *today*?" was her next question. "Tomorrow is the Sabbath and I'm getting ready!" It was a wonderful moment when Antonia realized the answer to her prayers for her. For Maria it was the beginning of faithful Sabbath keeping till the end of her life. She was baptized and became an Adventist in the refugee camp in Villach, Austria, after meeting up with that dear Adventist lady, Antonia.

Meanwhile Maria, with her two girls, was hoping to leave Europe for somewhere else. She couldn't return to Serbia, which at that time was in Soviet hands, and her husband was gone, probably for good. Some of her family had emigrated to Australia and others to South America. Eventually she and the girls were sponsored to come to America by the Yugoslavian Adventist church in Astoria, New York, on Long Island. That is where she met our dear lifelong friend, Ann Vitorovich, who now resides in Arizona. Ann's two books, *Any Way Out* and *Whom Shall I Fear* tell the exciting stories of her own family's escape from Yugoslavia. We recommend them highly.[19]

JIM'S FAMILY HERITAGE

After our meetings in Yugoslavia, we took a side trip to Sibiu, Romania, in the western area known as Siebenbürgen ("seven towns," or Transylvania), the ancestral home of my father's family. It was the result of a casual remark I made one day to a German Adventist pastor in Michigan, Edmund Grentz. I mentioned to him that our last name was originally Schwachhofer, and he said that he had known some people by that name in the "old country." So, I questioned, "Really? What 'old country'?" And he replied, "Transylvania." In fact, he said he could probably put me in touch with someone back in Sibiu, Romania, and also in Calgary, Alberta, Canada, who would provide information. Then an amazing series of miracles began. I wrote a letter to the Lutheran pastor in Sibiu and didn't hear from him for at least a couple of months. (All these Schwachhofers were Lutheran). But in several weeks a letter came, containing our family's history way back to 1778, when the Lutherans were expelled from Austria by Empress Maria Theresa, who was

---

[19] There are many more interesting details to Maria's story. For the full account, watch the video "Vera—My Story" at my website: https://lostarkseminar.com/sermon-extras.

Catholic, and deported to the hinterlands of Transylvania, now part of western Romania. Here is a copy of the letter I received, translated from German:

An Immigration Tragedy/200 Years Ago

The Story of a Family from Neppendorf

It was in the year 1778, exactly 20 years ago, during the reign of the very strict Catholic Empress Maria Theresia [of the Austria-Hungarian Empire], that for the final time so-called Protestants of the Alpine Steiermark region were herded together and deported from their beautiful homeland to Siebenbuergen [Transylvania]. The land where they would be sent was strange and unknown to them, almost as if you were to take someone today and move him from familiar surroundings to the South Pole.

Among these unfortunate but faithful Protestant believers there was a young couple from Obersteiermark, 26-year-old Josef Schwachhofer and his 27-year-old wife Anna, nee Wasserburger. They were the parents of a one-year-old daughter, Anna Maria. The young woman was very advanced in pregnancy at the time, as the Empress' soldiers knocked on the couple's front door. Disregarding that she would soon again be a mother, the soldiers ordered them to come with them.

Already the leaves were falling, and the nights were growing cold. They [no doubt along with many others] were probably put on a ship on the Danube river [where they would travel as far as what is now northern Yugoslavia], and then would travel by foot through Hungary and the Banat area, to their new home in Siebenbuergen. As the group arrived in Banat, however, another horrible incident occurred. As officers and soldiers of the Empress inspected the deportees, they especially took notice of the minor children. Mercilessly the soldiers snatched the children from their sides and the parents were forced to continue on their way without them. One-year-old Anna Maria Schwachhofer would be raised by Catholic foster parents in Karascher Komitat in the Lugosch region, today unknown. According to the state officials, the child must be removed from evangelical [Lutheran] influence and raised as a Catholic.

As they continued on their way from Banat to Hermannstadt [now Sibiu, Romania], the Schwachhofer parents encountered yet another hardship. During the journey—we don't know where—in the month of October Anna gave birth to a baby boy, whom they named Franz. Finally, they arrived in Hermannstadt, with their newborn son, but without their one-year-old daughter. We can only imagine what went on in their hearts, but we can't put it into words.

The deportees were directed to Josefsstadt, a village near Hermannstadt, where other immigrants were also assigned to live. Josef Schwachhofer, as a former resident of the forest lands, knew a lot about working with wood. He now earned his daily bread as a wood and coal worker. But this place wouldn't be where they stayed permanently. In 1783 they became part of the Neppendorf [now Turnisor, a western suburb of Sibiu] community. On the "old street" the Schwachhofers built themselves a home. And this is where the couple became the parents of two more daughters, Elisabeth and Rosina.

In 1780, however, Empress Maria Theresia died, and the following year her son and heir Emperor Josef II issued a decree of toleration. All Christian confessions were given limited religious freedom. This ended any further deportation and brutalities. All the Protestants who had been deported to Transylvania began to think about reuniting with the children that had been taken from them. Some of them even wrote to the Emperor's palace in Vienna—Josef Schwachhofer among them—and requested that their children be returned.

In the Neppendorf church archives there is a document that Josef Schwachhofer received as a result of his inquiry. The letter is dated August 22, 1786, when Anna Maria was already 9 years old. Emperor Josef II, despite his liberal mindset, was not willing in this case to reunite the children with their parents but would allow the parents to go wherever the children lived to have "a free and unrestricted conversation" with them. The local authorities were contacted, and arrangements were made for the Schwachhofers' arrival and departure. They were told that if they tried to talk to their child about religion they would be forbidden ever to talk to or see her again. The child was to remain Catholic. It is not known whether the parents ever made the long and difficult trip to Banat.

We do know that in 1792 in Neppendorf another child was added to the family, a little boy named Josef. The father died at the early age of 45 in 1797 in Neppendorf. According to the inheritance records, Anna Maria never did come to live with her parents, but grew up in Banat. So, we see then that the deportation and the taking away of the children was meant to be permanent.

The other children put down roots in Neppendorf. Elisabeth married Mathias "Penonre" Beer and Rosina married Mathias "Restl" Reisenauer, both strong, healthy families. To this day, many family members continue to live in Neppendorf. And both sons, Franz who was born on the journey, and the youngest, Josef, have passed on their family name Schwachhofer. Both married Landler women from Neppendorf and settled on the "old street," where many other Landlers reside, and a Landler village sector has developed.

So, this whole upper Austrian group, from the time of the first immigrations during the 1734-1738 era, has now blended together in Neppendorf [with the Saxons, who had lived there since the 12th century[20]], and their children will not ever be taken from them again.

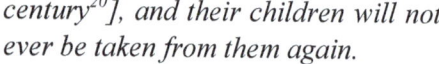

Franz Schwachhofer learned to be a tailor, and became the patriarch of that Schwachhofer branch, now nicknamed "Schneider" [tailor] to this day. The younger brother Josef became the patriarch of that Schwachhofer branch nicknamed "Lindner" [elm], supposedly because there were many linden trees on their farm.

Over 200 years have passed since the Schwachhofer family was deported from upper Austria under difficult circumstances. From immigrant Josef Schwachhofer, nine generations have lived and are still living in Neppendorf. There are 90 residents that are members of the Protestant [Evangelical Lutheran] church in Neppendorf that carry the name Schwachhofer, descendants of the families deported from Obersteiermark.

---

[20] https://www.britannica.com/topic/Transylvanian-Saxons

Their hold on the Gospel and the Protestant faith were so strong that they would give anything just to live free in their beliefs. It is gratifying that many of the offspring of these faithful believers still stand firm in the Gospel to this day. —Dr. Hellmut Klima [1915-1990], Neppendorf, 26 July 1978 [pastor, 1940-1980][21]

In Novi Sad we met a young Adventist physician, Dr. Branislav Hačko, a ham radio operator with the call sign YU7BH, and his wife Slavica. They live near the Romanian border in the town of Kikinda. He offered to put us up for the night and drive us across to the nearby town of Timişoara. There we would meet up with a young pastor who would be our guide for the weekend. Before leaving on that trip, we stopped by the family jewelry store, owned by his father. He offered us each the gift of a wristwatch, any watch we wished to choose from the store! And that's the watch I still wear every day. It's a chronometer watch, made by Fossil.

We spent a whole weekend in Sibiu, Romania, in the nearby village of Neppendorf, and in the town cemetery we were amazed to see some 40 gravestones reading "Schwachhofer." And in the little church we saw dolls dressed in the garb of those early days plus other historical materials, maps, genealogy charts, and the like. It was truly fascinating. I was able to copy details of the Schwachhofer genealogy from the church records. So, the Joseph mentioned earlier was my great-great-great grandfather, born in 1752. My grandfather Andreas, pictured on page 7, used the name Andrew Hoffer soon after he came to America, and had it legally changed in 1938. And I'm so glad he did! So, as you see, there are

---

[21] *www.landler.com/landler/intro/unverarbeitet/faminp.doc*

quite a few Hoffers in the United States, but we aren't related to any of them, unless they have a Schwachhofer in their ancestry.

We attended the Sibiu Adventist church that Sabbath, and in the congregation were several Gypsies in their special attire. It is wonderful that the Gospel is reaching so many different people groups. Wikipedia reveals that these "Roma" originated in the Punjab region of northern India as a nomadic people and entered Europe between the eighth and tenth centuries. They were called "Gypsies" because Europeans mistakenly believed they came from Egypt. They are now found in many other parts of the world. We had seen some even in South America.

On one of our trips to a ham radio meeting in 1991 in British Columbia, we afterward crossed the mountains to Calgary, Alberta, and visited Andrew and Maria Schwachhofer, the family in Canada whom Pastor Grentz had alerted us to. Amazingly one of his daughters there looked so much like my cousin Andrea! We were not able to trace our exact relationship though. The given name Andrew/ Andreas had been used many times.

WEDDING

On Sunday, November 24, 2002, I had the privilege of officiating at the wedding of Rick and his bride, Kelly Jo Schebo. On Saturday evening the 23rd, all were at the church for the rehearsal. The groom, the best man, and I stood on the platform, awaiting the entrance of the bridal party. The flower girl proceeded, pretending to scatter flower petals as she went. Next came the Bible boy, empty-handed, pretending to carry a Bible. So, I remarked, "Hmm, an invisible Bible." Without missing a beat, Michael Covarrubias, the best man, standing at my side, quipped, "Yes, it's *The Clear Word*!" And of course, everyone had a good laugh. Most Adventists are familiar with that very popular Bible paraphrase, written by Jack Blanco.

MISSION TRIPS TO BRAZIL AND URUGUAY

In Brazil (2003) and Uruguay (2004) we were reunited with dear friends and Vera's family. We experienced something sad in Brazil that year, much past tourist season. Driving along near the ocean, with no one around, we could see a small figure down on the beach. We stopped for a closer look. It turned out to be a penguin, hundreds and hundreds of miles from its home in the Antarctic. We picked it up and tossed it back in the water, but it immediately returned to shore. You see, it was covered from head to foot in petroleum! It would have drowned out there. We searched in vain for someone to help. Sadly, we had to leave it behind, and who knows what happened to it after that?

CLOSE CALLS

In 2004 God protected me from death no less than three times. Early in the year I was diagnosed with prostate cancer and underwent a robotic prostatectomy a few weeks before our mission trip. Despite that, we did not cancel going to Uruguay, and I was able to work hard there mixing and carrying cement despite my pain. Our mission team is pictured here. We spent nearly two weeks there completing a partly finished community service building and had a wonderful time.

In August we were at our booth at the Oshkosh Pathfinder camporee. On the opening day I had a serious choking episode while eating lunch at the back of our booth. Had not Vera noticed it, with hundreds of people milling around, and given me the Heimlich maneuver, I most certainly wouldn't have survived.

Then one night in December we were traveling home in heavy traffic from Rockville, Maryland, at about 60 m.p.h., and slammed into a huge box in front of us on highway 270. We swerved and dodged around it, with cars passing us on both sides, until we finally came to rest on the shoulder. We were shaken but not injured. It turned out to be a mattress box that must have just fallen off the back of a pickup. We got off at the nearest exit, thanked God for His protection, rested a bit, and then resumed our journey home.

The Hagerstown Seventh-day Adventist Church in Maryland had an annual tradition, a fund-raising yard sale for the public. Members and others donated items, some provided baked goods for sale, and the proceeds went for some special church project. The venue for the sale was always a prominent location along the main road through town, known as Dual Highway or Route 40. The lot slopes gently down to the road. The church chose that vacant lot so that it would be visible to the many passers-by.

At one of these sales a few years ago, a folding table with children's items included a large, inflated rubber ball. Of course, that caught the eye of a three-year old boy. He grabbed it and began kicking it around the area. Then he scampered after it as it rolled toward the highway. Almost everyone was preoccupied at the time and didn't notice the unfolding possible tragedy. Just then I saw this out of the corner of my eye and yelled "Stop!" in my loudest voice. Fortunately, the child stopped just in time, and the ball rolled out right in front of a rapidly passing car and was demolished. That little boy is now a handsome young man in his twenties. Whew!

In 2005 I retired from full-time ministry, probably partly due to lingering fatigue from my prostate surgery the previous year. Anyway, I had fulfilled all the requirements to receive the North American Division full retirement allowance, 41 unbroken years in only eight different locations. Shortly after that the Chesapeake Conference needed a part-time stipend pastor for a small startup group in the town of Smithsburg, where we lived, and I accepted. A couple of years later they added another small group, this one in Inwood, West Virginia, about 50 miles away. Both locations were positive and joyful experiences.

Vera and I always enjoyed the annual 5K Run/Walk on the grounds of the Review and Herald Publishing Association in Hagerstown. One year the famous Micheff Sisters trio was present and sang a special serenade for Vera.

In 2006 we went on a Reformation Tour to Germany with Pastor Don Schneider. It was fascinating how he compared the lives of two influential Germans, Hitler on the negative side, and Luther on the positive. We visited Berlin in a freezing January, followed by Wittenberg and other places of note.

In Luther's house, now a museum, we saw his pulpit robe in a glass case. It seemed rather short to me, having pictured Luther as that stalwart, asserting Reformer, I asked our guide, "How tall was Luther?" She responded, "Five feet, two inches." What a surprise!

With his wife, Marti, Don concluded the tour with an amazing Luther dramatization, as pictured above.

In 2007 we joined a European music tour out of Shenandoah Valley Academy. It included venues in Germany, Austria, and Czech Republic. We toured the Mauthausen Concentration camp near Munich, Bach's house in Vienna and the cemetery where many of the great musicians are buried, the beautiful Neuschwanstein castle in Bavaria, the site of *Sound of Music* in Austria, a salt mine in Salzburg, and a fantastic concert in Czech Republic. We also visited the Church of the Bones near Prague.[22] To our surprise we ran across an Adventist restaurant in downtown Prague known as Country Life.

One afternoon we were walking through lovely Salzburg and came to a farmers' market. One man had a large display of cheese. I saw some cheese with holes in it, and I remarked to Vera, "Oh, Swiss cheese!" And the man furrowed his brow and scowled at me, saying, "This is *Austria*!" in perfect English. Oops! In other words, don't you dare call this "Swiss" cheese here! I replied in German, "Wie kannst du so gut Englisch sprechen?" (How can you speak such good English?). And he replied, "I used to live in Chicago!"

---

[22] https://sedlecossuary.com

MY CHILDREN AS ADULTS

Barbara Battle is a certified high school Spanish teacher in Massachusetts. She loves outdoor activity and raises a huge garden, providing lots of fresh food for her family. Her husband, **Michael**, is a financial analyst working for Avid Technology Inc. Together, they are also area coordinators for the Pathfinder and Adventurer ministries in the Southern New England Conference of Seventh-day Adventists and active in their church. Their children are **Sofia**, **Natalie,** and **Dimitri**.

Tamara Hoffer is a professional corporate and editorial freelance photographer, also currently working as an IT project manager for a denominational insurance organization. She inherited the travel bug and enjoys visiting friends and new places within the US and overseas.

Barbara and Tamara are both multilingual, having lived in South America. The other children were quite young when we returned, so they have pretty much lost touch with Spanish and Portuguese. In addition, Barbara spent a college year in Spain, and Tamara in France.

Michele Pokuta and her husband, **Joseph** have owned and operated a successful boat dealership near the shores of Lake Michigan since 1995. They are raising their two teenage children, **Joey** and **Jennifer** and doing their best to keep all the balls in the air as they manage their busy life. Joe is an avid outdoorsman who enjoys hunting and fishing and Michele, also an outdoors person, appreciates nature through paddle boarding, hiking, and yard work. Both kids enjoy time at the lake. Jennifer has a strong creative side and enjoys writing and painting. Joey spends his spare time creating computer games for his friends to play.

Richard Hoffer and his wife, **Kelly**, have both worked as certified schoolteachers. However, Rick is currently working as a journeyman commercial carpenter in Minnesota. Kelly home schools their three daughters, **Sami**, **Madi**, and **Ruthi** and works part-time. The girls enjoy  their mini city farm consisting of two dogs, one cat, three rabbits, a hamster, and a gerbil. They enjoy spending time with family and friends and being in the great outdoors.

VERA AND HER SEWING HOBBY

Vera had always been a wonderful and talented seamstress, making clothes for the children and outfits for herself. She had even made her own wedding dress. As she was getting closer to retirement from nursing, she went back to sewing and added machine embroidery to her repertoire. Her work was absolutely beautiful. We began to attend craft fairs, such as one near Chicago in Itasca, Illinois, where she could display and sell her wares. That was one of the "juried" craft fairs, where one's work is first judged worthy before it is allowed to be displayed. We also took her dolls and other items to many hamfests, so she and I were selling things alongside each other. One year at the Dayton (Ohio) Hamvention her Raggedy Anns and sock dolls brought in over $750.00! We kept up with this activity until moving to Ringgold, Georgia, in 2011.

Our children put on a riotously funny birthday party for Vera's 65th, using a pirate theme. She was called "The great pirate Oh!" The other members of the fleet were Wah, Tah, Goo, Si, and Am. Get it? It was held at Michele and Joe's previous house in Indiana. They followed with a 70th for me and a 70th for her, and perhaps others I am not covering here. I am proud of my wonderful, talented children.

In 2010 Vera and I joined with Dr. Gerard Damsteegt and his wife, Laurel, on a study tour of Europe known as the Great Controversy Tour.[23] They run this at least once every summer and I highly recommend it. The tour follows the Protestant Reformation from Rome to Florence and Bobbio Pellice in the northwest mountains near France, plus places in Geneva and other locations. We saw all the sites, both pagan and Christian, and enjoyed 12 days of touring and study. We went to Italy, Switzerland, Germany, and France. Our last stop was Paris and the Eiffel Tower.

After that experience I wrote: "Many have had the privilege of participating in the Great Controversy Tour with Dr. and Mrs. Gerard Damsteegt of the Theological Seminary at Andrews University. It is an awesome experience to see history up close and personal, visiting Rome, Geneva, Zurich, Konstanz, Paris, and other Reformation sites. Probably the most impressive sites include the Colosseum, where many Christians were fed to the lions or burned at the stake; the cave in northern Italy, where many Waldensian Protestants were hunted down and killed; and Konstanz, site of the burning at the stake of both Hus and Jerome. To be standing at those very spots is an immensely moving moment. There was virtually no religious liberty in those dark days. Of course, these dedicated believers were only following in the footsteps of their Savior, who was tortured and died on the cross, becoming the supreme sacrifice of all time."

---

[23] For further information, contact Laurel at laurelatlast@me.com.

On November 16, 2003, Sunshine, a sun conure (*Aratinga solstitialis*), came to bless our home through a friend at the Hagerstown church. Sunshine had been born (hatched) on March 8, 1987.

During this five-year period, I also worked part-time for the Review and Herald Publishing Company, as a contract proofreader and copy editor.

Later in 2010 we announced our full retirement. I had turned 70 and we felt it was time to move to a warmer climate, especially after a very hard winter. Looking around, we settled on Ringgold, Georgia, just south of the campus of Southern Adventist University in Collegedale, Tennessee, for the next chapter of our lives.

As mentioned before, my father died in 2000, and was buried in Brooklyn Heights cemetery near Cleveland, Ohio. Vera's mother died in 2001, and was buried in New Buffalo, Michigan, just a walking distance from Michele and Joe's marine service business. My mother died in 2010 and was buried next to Dad. Now *we* were the patriarchs of the family!

RINGGOLD, GEORGIA

The town of Ringgold, population 3,700, is located near Chattanooga, Tennessee, and sits about 10 miles from the campus of Southern Adventist University. One of its distinguishing features is the old railroad depot at the south end of town, and the underpass next to it on highway US 41. Before the construction of Interstate 75, US 41 was the only road through the area on the way to Dalton, Calhoun, Atlanta, and points south.

The problem was, and still is, that the railroad underpass there has very low clearance—only 11 feet, 7 inches. Large vehicles such as semis cannot pass through. There are warning signs everywhere regarding the detour around it with bright yellow signs, flashing lights, dangling objects, etc. Invariably, two or three times a year a truck driver will ignore or not notice the signage and plow into the bridge. The result is a heavily damaged truck, a fine of $10,000, and a blocked roadway for several hours while the mess is being cleaned up!

Anyway, that was our town, and we enjoyed our seven years at 1894 Salem Valley Road. We moved in around March 1, 2011.

Vera and I became members of Master Chorale, an adult traveling choir of about 25 or 30, directed by Dr. Bruce Ashton, my friend from childhood.

Seven weeks later, on April 27, a Wednesday evening, a terrible tornado passed through the area during one of our rehearsals on the campus of the university. Though it was very close, we didn't know about it or hear it from inside the music building. When we attempted to return the 10 miles to our house, many roads were totally blocked by debris and emergency vehicles. It took us over an hour to navigate alternate roads in total darkness, as there were no lights anywhere. We didn't realize it had been a tornado until the next morning. It missed our home by about half a mile. Later we were able to

drive around the area, but the devastation was horrible. One house not too far away from us took a direct hit, killing all six people inside. A few of the professors at the university lost their homes completely.

We enjoyed our new home and joined the McDonald Road Seventh-day Adventist church in McDonald, Tennessee, where we made many new friends.

MY FIRST BOOK

During the time I was pastoring the Smithsburg group, we had come up with several forms of outreach to the community, such as Bible seminars and health ministry. Near the time of our leaving, I had begun to think of a unique Bible seminar based on what Adventists call the "sanctuary message." I started to sketch out a plan, but because we were so busy, I never completed it.

At some point during our time at the McDonald Road Church, my seminar idea returned, and I began to write. I came up with a series of 12 lessons based on the ancient Hebrew sanctuary and all that it signified in the ministry of Christ. The sanctuary is really a fascinating study. Since our church already had Wednesday night Bible study, I requested permission to teach my new seminar as a pilot program. It was very well received, and after polishing it up some, I decided to have it published. I chose an Adventist publisher nearby, TEACH Services, and it came out in November 2014. Then I began to seek venues at which to share it—other churches, camp meetings, etc.

Beginning in 2015 I presented it in several churches, and in the camp meetings of the Georgia-Cumberland and Michigan conferences. (A camp meeting is an annual summer convocation, a long weekend or sometimes lasting up to 10 days.) In subsequent years, up until Covid-19, I presented at many individual churches and at camp meetings in conferences such as Kentucky-Tennessee, Indiana, Southern New England, Pennsylvania, Mountain View (West Virginia), and Wisconsin.

By this time, I had translated my book into both Spanish and Portuguese, too. In early 2019 I traveled to Brazil and spoke in two churches, one in the north (Uberlândia, Minas Gerais) and one in the south (Tubarão, Santa Catarina). Now the book is also available in French.

Of course, it needed and I designed a special website, www.LostArkSeminar.com, where my book and other products are offered for sale, with helps for instructors and others. It has been quite a ride, and nothing I ever foresaw when I began. As of this writing I have sold nearly 3,000 copies and presented many, many seminars.

We had a singular experience at the Pennsylvania camp meeting, held annually on the campus of Blue Mountain Academy near the town of Hamburg. One day at our hotel, a bearded man came limping in. Turns out he had been hiking on the Appalachian Trail, which follows a ridge across the road from the academy and had made it all the way from the southern terminus in his home state of Georgia. A couple of days prior, he had slipped on a wet rock going through Maryland and severely hurt his left leg. Determined to finish his goal of walking the AT, he continued as far as Hamburg. By now, though, it was too bad to continue the trail without medical help. We took him under our wings. We drove him to Walmart to buy some Epsom salts to soak his leg in the tub. That bought him a little time. We also took him around the campus. There he saw some posters about the meetings. He saw a picture of Doug Batchelor and said, "I know that man! I watch him all the time!" (Doug is one of our Adventist TV evangelists.)

But it turned out not to be enough. We drove him to a local clinic. There he was x-rayed, and the results were that the bone was broken! It was not a compound fracture, so the doctor wrapped it tightly. But now he had to alter his plan. He finally rented a car and drove home to Georgia. The following year he resumed his trek and completed it. But now we had a new Christian friend, and we are still in touch with him, Dwight Davis. His "trail name" is Sleeves.

VERA'S HEALTH

This is now the saddest event of my life. In December of 2012, Vera discovered a lump in her left breast. We immediately sought out a specialist, and sure enough, it was malignant. She soon began radiation and chemotherapy treatments, and eventually had a left mastectomy. The next three and a half years were frightful—her health up and down constantly. Times of hope and times of fear. We both suffered, but in different ways. The children and family were very supportive. Vera was a very brave woman; despite her condition she still loved life and traveled with me everywhere until she couldn't. She was a wonderful people-person, even in times of pain. And spiritually, she *never* said "Why me?" or complained to God. She rather said, "Why not me?"

Our house in Ringgold had a split foyer entry, and no matter how weak she was, stairs had to be climbed whenever we returned home from shopping or the hospital. Often it would take many minutes to help her up the stairs, sitting on a step and taking one at a time. Eventually she was wheelchair-bound. Finally, the time came for hospice care, with a special bed brought in. The hospice people were super nice and caring, wonderful to work with.

I spent much time those last few days at her bedside, and was with her when she breathed her last, on June 14, 2016. It was just two weeks after her 74th birthday on May 29 and four days short of our 55th anniversary. She was buried in the Collegedale, Tennessee, cemetery, and a memorial service followed at our McDonald Road church on June 25. The headstone has both our names on it. When I join her in death someday, my date of death will be added.

My brother Bill rendered the following tribute at Vera's memorial service:

I first got to know Vera and her sister Olga during a few events that were shared by the youth groups of Lakewood Seventh-day Adventist church and the Adventist church on the east side of Cleveland. We became more acquainted during Vera's senior year and my junior year at Mount Vernon Academy, the Adventists' boarding high school in central Ohio. Vera and I occasionally crossed paths on the meandering walkways of the campus, and we always shared a pleasant greeting. One day late in the school year when we encountered each other once again, I was perplexed to see that her entire face was swollen well out of proportion. She saw my look of surprise and mumbled that she had just had her "...wizzm...teesh...pult...oud."

Soon after that enlightening conversation we returned to our respective homes in Cleveland for summer vacation. And early that summer our Lakewood church hosted a youth group roller skating party in the basement recreational area of the building. I remember the occasion well, because the date was June 11, my birthday.

Jim remembers the date also, but for another reason.

My older brother was also back in Cleveland for a break in his studies as a theology major at what was then known as Columbia Union College in Takoma Park, Maryland. As fate would have it, he and I attended the skating party together, where young men and women were whirling about the floor to the quiet serenade of recorded music. It did not take long for Jim to notice a pretty young blonde girl in the crowd, and I happened to see that her facial swelling had subsided completely. After a few minutes of staring across the room at the girl Jim asked me who she was. I told him her name was Vera and I walked him over to the blonde girl and introduced them to one another. Jim wasted no time asking Vera if she would like to skate with him and for the next hour or so I watched their skates spinning non-stop around the basement floor. Or was it their hearts that were spinning?

Then and there I witnessed the beginning of an epic love story. Vera and Jim went on to skate through their lives together and in future years they always celebrated my birthday as a very special event. Their marriage continued for almost 55 years, but the love story does not end there, for we know with certainty that they will be skating together throughout eternity.

(Bill's view differs a bit with what I remember about how Vera and I met. But at this point it doesn't matter.)

I confess that I was shocked, numb, and extremely lonely after her death. The silence in our home was deafening. As I began to go through her things, I spent much of the time wondering what the future might hold for me. And I spent *much* time in prayer. Grief is managed by people in many different ways. My way was to stay busy. Now every duty was mine. Cooking, cleaning, doing laundry and yard work—my helpmeet was gone. The graveyard was only minutes from our house, so I would often go there to think and ponder and pray.

As my spirits started to lift, I began to consider the future. I felt such an emptiness, but I had seen others make poor and hasty decisions regarding remarriage. My prayer at that point was, "Lord, don't let me do something foolish like seek a mate on the Internet. If it is Your will for me, please just bring someone into my life. I want You to handle this." And He did.

WEDDING BELLS AGAIN

Ruth Wright and I had gone to college together in Takoma Park, Maryland, and knew each other only slightly. But through the years, circumstances would bring about a reconnection. During the time I was pastoring in Hagerstown, Ruth's husband Ken Wright was assisting at a branch bookstore for the Adventist Book Center in Silver Spring,  Maryland. This branch was located in Hagerstown, on the campus of Highland View Academy, just a few miles from our home in Smithsburg. Coincidentally, her mother, Esther Miller, had been a member of my Hagerstown church, so I would run into them occasionally.

On Sabbath, April 30, 2016, Ruth was visiting one Sabbath at the McDonald Road church. Her husband had passed away a few years earlier, in 2011. I happened to see her sitting a few rows ahead of me (big church, about a thousand members, with two worship services every Sabbath). After the service we spoke briefly with each other and exchanged email addresses. And that was that.

We emailed each other a couple of times in June, because one of my amateur radio friends, Carroll Chickering, W3HHS, lived near her and had lost his antennas in a storm. He was also having health issues, so we talked about that. After Vera had died on June 14, she sent me a nice message of condolences. None of this had any implications of a deeper friendship. Anyway, that wouldn't have been appropriate at that time in the least.

I was able to get an appointment with the Chesapeake Conference to make a presentation regarding my sanctuary seminar at their pastors' meeting on September 20, so I also offered to preach at Berkeley Springs on the 17th. Later, Ruth invited me to come for her church's annual "outdoor church," which I gladly accepted. Anytime I came I spent the night at Lee Wilson's house on Pious Ridge Road. After Lee passed away, Ruth's neighbor Barney Hill accommodated me. Delightfully, he later became an Adventist and joined our church.

The friendship grew warmer with the passing of time. Ruth came down my way a few times as well, since she had family in Calhoun, Georgia, not far away. She often spent the night at the home of our friends Jim and Linda Albertson, whom we had both known back in college.

Again, in January 2017 she came to Georgia for a wedding. On an unusually warm January day, the 12th, we went for a walk in a nearby park. Heading back toward my car, we sat for a bit on a nice park bench. It was then that I proposed. She responded, "Jim, I just can't tell you right now." I said that that was okay, I understood. Then I drove her to Atlanta to catch her plane home, a two-hour trip from Ringgold, and little was spoken. She must have been thinking deeply and praying, because as I pulled up to the curb at the departure area and placed her suitcase on the sidewalk, she said, "Jim, the answer is yes!" and gave me a nice kiss. Then she turned, picked up the suitcase, and was gone, just like that. I was totally on cloud 9 then and hardly could believe my ears. I don't even remember the drive home.

Now there were many phone calls, emails, and further visits back and forth. We set a date of April 2 for the wedding. I decided to sell my Georgia home and move up north to her home. Now *I* had a home to clean out and sell, but God had a plan for that too. The only other negative was that I would need to give up Pepper and Sunshine, but I adjusted to that also and gave them to some friends from the McDonald Road church.

As of this writing, Pepper is still doing well and is being cared for by my friends, but Sunshine died on September 9, 2019.[24]

In the town of East Ridge, a suburb on the south side of Chattanooga, there is a wonderful flea market. For only $10 a space on Sundays I could pull up with my trailer and sell off my goods. Much of Vera's vast inventory of fabrics and sewing supplies went that way. Her expensive embroidery machines were sold on Craig's list and through eBay. A local sewing shop bought her steel shelving and a large table that I had made. And so it went.

Prior to our actual wedding, we were counseled by her pastor, Jason Disch, using the Prepare-Enrich testing instrument from a Christian marriage counseling company in Minnesota. We had to take the test totally independently on our computers. When we got together with Pastor Jason, the first thing he said was, "By any chance, did you guys cheat on this test?" We replied, "Absolutely not." Then he said, "You folks have the highest compatibility score I have ever seen in my whole counseling experience!" He was amazed and so were we. I guess that's why our marriage is so strong.

We had a lovely wedding at the Berkeley Springs church, officiated by Pastor Disch, on Sunday, April 2. Afterward we left for our honeymoon, spending our first night at a bed and breakfast (her son Kenneth's wedding gift to us) in Luray, Virginia. The following day we enjoyed the beautiful caverns. We drove down into southwest Georgia then, because we were planning to visit Callaway Gardens. After a long tiring drive, we found it closed, due to severe weather threatening the area. It would have to wait for another day, another year.

---

[24] For a cute video about Sunshine" on my website:
https://lostarkseminar/sermon-extras

So, about the house to sell, now what? An Adventist couple in Michigan, old friends from Mount Vernon Academy and classmates of Vera, were looking for a house in that area. Their son worked at McKee Foods Corporation, in Collegedale, Tennessee, the nearby home of Little Debbies. I showed them the house and they loved it. A few weeks later we settled at the local closing office—no realtor, no financing either, just cash. God is so good.

Ruth and I settled in to the work of the church in Berkeley Springs. We both love to visit and encourage people, so we do that often. We sing duets for special music, she is the volunteer secretary, and I am one of the elders. Currently, among my duties is conducting prayer meeting, attending church board meetings, being platform chairman three times a year, and occasional preaching.

In early 2019 I was called by the Chesapeake Conference to be interim pastor for the Williamsport, Maryland, church, with around 400 members. They had recently lost their pastor. That stint lasted for about five months. By the way, many of my sermons from there are on YouTube. Just type in "James R Hoffer" to have a look. Interestingly, Pastor Elmer Malcolm, whom we mentioned earlier as pastor of the Battle Creek Tabernacle, now retired, was a member of that church. It was nice to see him again after so many years. He passed away in January of 2021.

We have taken many trips, including a visit to Noah's Ark in northern Kentucky; Colonial Village in Williamsburg, Virginia; Sight and Sound Theater in Lancaster, Pennsylvania; and my various speaking appointments.

Ruth and I have a wonderful marriage, and our respective children have been very supportive and accepting of us as a couple. My eight grandchildren love their new "grandma," and she loves them too. We have loving families on both sides.

We are avid recyclers, and frequently clean up roadsides in our area, especially certain side roads near us. We have also paid for and posted signs on large trees here and there, saying "PLEASE NO TRASH." Would you believe it? Some people are so offended by these reminders that they tear down the signs! This happens particularly in one area where young people love to park on weekend nights. Wonder what *they're* up to?

A humorous event occurred before my very eyes one summer evening. I pulled up to a traffic light and another car pulled up behind me. I noticed in my rearview mirror that they threw out some trash from both sides of their car. What they didn't know was that right behind them was a police car! He called out to them through his megaphone, "Do you folks happen to have an extra $500 to pay for this deed?" They immediately sprang from their car, picked up the trash, and sheepishly pulled away when the light turned green. I just laughed and laughed.

Another of our passions is the game of Scrabble™. We try to play it at least once every day. We score high and mostly evenly because we are both literary people.

Once Ruth and I were at a funeral in Winchester, Virginia, about an hour south of our home in Berkeley Springs, West Virginia. The Pentecostal minister spoke about the resurrection and quoted from 1 Corinthians 15:51-52: "Behold, I show you a mystery; we shall not all sleep, but we shall all be changed, in a moment, in the twinkling of an eye..." and he stopped and said, "See folks, 'absent from the body and present with the Lord,'" suggesting that we go right to heaven when we die. I was shocked! It was all I could do to remain in my seat. He deliberately chopped off the last part of verse 52, which reads "*at the last trump*: for the trumpet shall sound, and the dead shall be raised incorruptible, and we shall be changed." As the parables of Matthew 13 attest, there can be no resurrection of the dead *until after the judgment day*, and *only then* occurs the "harvest." The whole world has bought Satan's lie in the Garden of Eden, "Ye shall not surely die," and that concept is found in almost every religion of the world. How could we go to reward or punishment before we are judged? It doesn't make sense. And *nowhere* in the Bible is the term "immortal soul" to be found. Clearly, the Bible teaches "soul sleep."[25]

CUBA

In mid-November 2017 we traveled to Cuba, sponsored by Quiet Hour Ministries in California. We arrived at the Holguín airport on the afternoon of the 15th. Holguín is situated about 450 miles east of the capital, Havana. It was a most wonderful experience for our team. There were five venues in the area, preaching, working with the children, giving health talks, and during the day ministering to the people. We had taken with us 1,500 pairs of donated reading glasses of various strengths to distribute, crafts for the vacation Bible school, and suitcases full of used clothing. We also took

---

[25] For additional information, see chapter 9 in my book, *Secrets and Mysteries of the Lost Ark* and if possible, watch the outstanding film, *Hell and Mr. Fudge*.

blood pressures. As we distributed the glasses, people were asked to read a selected passage from the Bible.

The conference president was Eber Delgado, and our little group consisted of Ruth and me and Michael Case. The others from our team were assigned to other venues. Each night as I preached in the main sanctuary, Ruth and Michael were with the children, Ruth conducting a VBS-type program, and Michael assigned to giving health talks as well as helping with the children. They had a translator, an Adventist English professor from the area.

Pictured above we are gathered at the highest point in town, La Loma de la Cruz (Hill of the Cross). Most of the team were from the U.S., but there was a young man from Nicaragua and a lady from Jamaica.

The streets of Holguín were very clean, and we saw many well-kept old cars and the occasional horse-drawn taxi. There were many nice homes, lesser ones right beside them. All houses are built right up to the sidewalk, as in many other countries. Pretty good Internet and cell phone service was available in the city park.

One day we went to the site where Christopher Columbus landed in 1492. We were treated to a drink of coconut water right from the shell. The host cut off the tops with his machete and we were given straws. There was a little park with grass huts, and under a roof were artifacts from an archaeological dig. The guide explained that the recent hurricane had taken much of the beachfront.

On Thanksgiving Day, our group had a special treat. Our sponsors, the Quiet Hour, hired a bus to take us, the local pastors and their families, and the conference staff to a beautiful beach resort called The Breezes. It was a lovely place by the ocean with a large pool. A big hotel catered to tourists and we chatted with some from other countries that have no restrictions for visiting Cuba.

Several baptisms, a baby dedication, and beautiful choral music took place at the final evening meeting. In this island nation, there are 328 Seventh-day Adventist churches with over 34,000 members. Before we left on the last Sabbath, I donated my laptop and projector to our Alcides Pino church.

Our flight home was scheduled for Monday, November 27, but as we sat on the plane the pilot reported a problem with the computer. We had to return to the airport until they could bring in another plane some eight hours later. We finally arrived home the next day, very tired but grateful for the wonderful mission experience.

COLORADO

Thanks to Ruth's son, Kenneth, we celebrated her 77th birthday in 2019 at his mountain home in Gypsum, Colorado. Both weather and scenery were beautiful and refreshing. We enjoyed long walks, a visit to the Betty Ford Alpine Garden, and a four-hour horseback trip.

In those delightful moments, little did we know that 2020 would bring in its train health problems for me, and the worldwide Covid-19 pandemic.

MY HEALTH ISSUES

In January 2020 what was supposed to be a routine wellness checkup turned scary. As mentioned earlier, I had had a prostatectomy in 2004, followed by radiation in 2006, which kept my PSA extremely low for all those years, as annual testing showed. This time it was definitely rising. Why now? Something weird was happening inside my body. Our doctor sent me to two cancer specialists in Hagerstown, a urologist and an oncologist. Both wanted to treat me with hormone therapy, what is termed androgen suppression therapy. The idea is to administer the female hormone estrogen to counteract the testosterone in men who have this problem. But the side effects can be difficult. We left those offices without committing to the therapy and began to pray about my situation. Our thoughts immediately went to Wildwood.[26]

---

[26] https://wildwoodhealth.com

To some degree we were always living healthfully. About the time that Barbie was born, Vera and I had decided to become vegetarians. Ruth and Ken were also vegetarians. It has been very beneficial to all of us. Wildwood added dimensions to that that we had never imagined.

Wildwood Lifestyle Center, located in north Georgia just below Chattanooga, Tennessee, with 700 acres of beautiful rolling hills, a large lake, and wonderful people, is renowned for its treatment of disease using natural remedies. It is not at all inexpensive, but we chose to sacrifice and go there for four weeks of treatment. (By the way, we had paid off our mortgage earlier.) The lifestyle changes are drastic, but certainly not impossible. Hydrotherapy, exercise, fruit smoothies, raw veggie juices, immunity teas, special supplements, use of charcoal, special diets, etc., are all designed to boost one's immune system. Now I am almost totally vegan, non-GMO, mostly organic, totally abstaining from sugar, and walking every day. My weight has returned to what I weighed back when I married Vera. I have tons of energy and am not lacking one bit in strength. The PSA has subsided somewhat, and I am hopeful. So far, so good. Anyway, the issue is about quality of life, isn't it? I am just truly sorry we couldn't have gone this route with Vera. It might have made a difference.

IN CONCLUSION

As I write these final lines, my stage 4 prostate cancer has been confirmed, despite the regimen I have faithfully followed for six months. My PET scans have revealed small but growing cancerous lesions in some of my bones. I am now on the hormone therapy prescribed by my oncologist. What next? Who knows? But after all, life is tenuous for us all, and it is better to be prepared for whatever eventuality. I do know this—the Wildwood experience has been tremendously beneficial, if only in terms of needed weight loss and the strengthening of my body. I haven't felt this well in years.

On September 26, 2020, I had the joyous privilege of baptizing three of my granddaughters, Samantha, Madeline, and Ruthann Hoffer, children of Rick and Kelly, in Rice Lake at North Star Camp in Brainerd, Minnesota. About 40 people—friends and church family—came for the Sabbath baptism at the church youth camp. Drizzling rain greeted us during the short service in the beautiful new camp lodge, after which all ate their own lunches. Just before the afternoon baptism, the sun came out and shone on Ruthi, 9; Madi, 13; and Sami, 15; as they met Grandpa in the chilly water. Someone had brought me a pair of chest-high waders, so I didn't feel it, but we all heard the squeal from Ruthi when she entered the chilly water! What a joy to see these young ladies give their hearts to Jesus.

This was undoubtedly one of the highlights of my "Grandpa" life. As I expressed to these three precious girls, during my many years as a pastor I have baptized hundreds of people and performed numerous weddings. Yet despite vows and pledges of faithfulness, some have since turned their backs on God, leaving the church or breaking marital relationships. How sad! This got me to thinking….

My 80-year lifespan has seen major changes and even upheavals in the world—World War II and wars in Korea, Vietnam, and the Middle East; the assassination of President John F. Kennedy; the walk on the moon; the computer age and the Internet; huge fires, tornadoes, hurricanes, and other natural disasters; the Covid-19 pandemic; and on a personal level, a tornado, a housefire, my cancer, and the passing of my first wife. On a couple of occasions, I was even treated poorly by a couple of church authorities. And yet, through it all, God has led and guided in a marvelous way. It puts me in mind of this Scripture verse: "Weeping may endure for a night, but joy cometh in the morning," (Psalm 30:5). My confidence in God has never wavered.

My mother's sentiments about our family were expressed so well in a letter she wrote us, penned in that same beautiful cursive and dated November 6, 1996: *"Every day I thank God for the beautiful flock He has given us. Words cannot express adequately how much we love you."*

And I cannot finish these memoirs without leaving an appeal to each of you:

Dear reader: Hopefully, you have seen through the stories in these pages how God guides us when we have given our lives to Jesus. *Please make sure you are totally committed to Jesus and His Word.* This life means *nothing* if we are not ready for eternity. I can't stress this enough. As I write this, I may have a year or two left, but more importantly, I want to see each of you in heaven someday. I love you all and pray that we will all be in attendance at that great "family reunion" to come!

"For the grace of God that bringeth salvation hath appeared to all men, teaching us that, denying ungodliness and worldly lusts, we should live soberly, righteously, and godly, in this present world; looking for that blessed hope, and the glorious appearing of the great God and our Saviour Jesus Christ; who gave himself for us, that he might redeem us from all iniquity, and purify unto himself a peculiar people, zealous of good works." —Titus 2:11-14

Poetry follows…

The Sanctuary
(Published in Renewed and Ready, *May 2010.)*
With tender care I planted there
A refuge and a haven.
I pulled much weed, I sowed much seed,
I visualized my Eden.

At last—'twas done! and growth begun
Of plant and flower and verdure.
With joyful air I breathed a prayer
For contemplated nurture.

Stand by! Give place! Behold the race,
As countless individuals
At once apprize and recognize
The likelihood of victuals.

Look now—forsooth! as claw and tooth
Of creatures bold, yet wary,
With omnivorous ecstasy
Now grace my sanctuary.

O coleopterous canticle!
O lagomorphic ballad!
O hark the ring of paw and wing
Descending on the salad!

Ye creatures wild, so meek, so mild,
I pause to beg your pardon—
That sacred ground that you have found
Was meant to be my garden!

Its vs. It's (5/4/1997)
(Published partially by Roland Hegstad several years ago in one of his religious liberty papers. And Dave Barry commented, quite appropriately, "Thank's for sending in you're poem.")

How it giveth me the fit's
To see how people spelleth "it's."
Doesn't anybody know
Where apostrophe's should go?
And it send's me up a wall

When some self-styled know-it-all
(Leaving egg on his own face)
Put's apostrophe's in place's
Where they have no business being.

Pretty soon we will be seeing
"Their's" and "your's" and "hi's" and "her's,"
And sundry other kind's of slur's.
Yes, it drive's me to distraction,
This abuse of a contraction
Oft confused with a possessive.

Seem's like some folk's are obsessive
To portray themselve's so literate,
That they end up like an idiot.
For depending on intentions,
Apostrophic interventions,
Here's the rule to put in action:
"NO possessive, YES contraction."

To avoid this mass confusion,
I propose a quick solution:
Let's alleviate frustration,
And get rid of punctuation.
It should make us stop and think
Just how many ton's of ink
We could save to our good pleasure
If we took this drastic measure.
Thank's to all the ignorami,
Certainly it's a shame. I
Wonder when it all will stop.
Guess we need a grammar cop!

Homeless for the Holidays
(Written during the recession, 2008; to the tune of "Home for the Holidays.")
We would love to be home for the holidays,
But a big yellow sign is on the door.
Freddie Mac took it back for the holidays,
So, we're sleeping in Mom's basement on the floor.

From the suburbs to the cities
Down to Dixie's sunny shore.
From Atlantic to Pacific
The foreclosures are prolific.

Oh, there's no place like home for the holidays,
How I wish so that we could still be there,
But the bank couldn't give us just a few more days,
So, we're on the street with nothing but a prayer.

From the shelter to the mission,
The soup kitchen now and then.
We just knew we'd be in trouble
When it broke—that housing bubble.

Yes, there's no place like home for the holidays,
Trouble is, we defaulted on our loan.
Here we are, poor and homeless for the holidays,
It's not fun to be kicked out of "home, sweet home."

Things were fine in Pennsylvania
While the mortgage rates were low.
Yes, we bought so big and greedy
Now we're feeling tight and needy.

We would love to be home for the holidays,
But a big yellow sign is on the door.
Freddie Mac took it back for the holidays,
So, we're sleeping in Mom's basement on the floor.

A Parable
I had a dream the other night,
It seemed so very true.
I stood beside my garden plot—
Some planting I would do.

I took a tiny little seed
And planted it with toil.
I placed it in the hole I'd made
There in the fertile soil.

What pleasure to cooperate
With heaven's all-wise plan! —
As I would hoe and rake and weed,
While God sent sun and rain.

Before too many days had passed
A tender shoot appeared—
A promise of abundant fruit
When harvest time should near.

Alas! Just 'fore maturity
A strange thing came about:
The plant decided on its own
To follow its own route.

Ignoring wiser thoughts and plans
It wriggled from its berth,
And one by one its roots drew out,
Till dying, fell to earth.

All in the name of freedom 'twas,
God's better plan to doubt.
The <u>only</u> source of life and joy
The little plant shut out.

Now plants don't have minds of their own,
Nor feet to walk untrue.
Too bad that thus plants show more trust
Than human beings do.

If plants <u>could</u> walk, would they submit
To that which God ordains?
Are plants then, more intelligent
Than people who have brains?

How wonderful to trust in God—
In <u>truest</u> sense be free,
Fulfilling in one's very life
Eternal destiny!

From Ruth

(My second wife, Ruth, wrote this during our dating time. The first time I proposed, a little prematurely, her response was "We'll see!")

There once was an impatient swain
Who found to his chagrin and pain,
That the one he would wed
Was reluctant instead
And "We'll see" was her constant refrain.

To Ruth

(My response, not to be outdone.)
This hapless old swain knows it's true
That someday his Ruth will come through.
Right now, he can't wait
For that magical date
When "We'll see" turns into "I do!"

Class Reunion

(Written around 2000 for Vera's 40th class reunion.)
Whether single or married,
Divorced or nearly buried…

A little less hair, or a little more tummy,
Or your life has turned out kinda crummy…

Or success has put you out of touch,
And you don't want to be with 'ordinary folks' much…

Or you feel funny to have to say
That you're no longer an SDA…

Whatever the reason, whatever excuse,
At this special time, don't be a recluse…

We ALL have our hang-ups and problems, it's true, but
THE REUNION WON'T BE THE SAME WITHOUT YOU!

Slug vs. Mouse

(Background: My first wife, Vera, was an avid and talented seamstress and machine embroiderer, and often worked on her projects late into the night. She was the "bear" and I was the "slug" ever since that poetry contest.)

Sad slug, lost his bear,
Couldn't find her anywhere.
Looked in bedroom, but not there,
Then he sees her in her chair.
Hour by hour downloads designs
While poor sluggy weeps and pines.
"Gotta check my e-mail, Hon."
But poor sluggy's day is done.
Tries to read until she comes.
To the sandman soon succumbs.
Exhausted by the day's demands,
Wants so much to hold her hands.
Kiss her, hug her, but instead,
Falls asleep in empty bed.
Constantly the bear indulges,
While the hard drive groans and bulges.
Many projects big and small,
Go undone and line the wall.
Unread magazines and books,
Fill up baskets, shelves, and nooks.
Can it be that in our house
Slug has been replaced by mouse?

Annals of the Great Limerick War
(*Jim wrote a few limericks for the Benton Harbor Library limerick contest in December 1989 and won the contest. The prize? The slug beanbag pictured above. Then he sent it and a couple of others to Bill. Bill, not to be outdone, replied. The Great Limerick War was on and continued for about a year.*)
Jim, December 1989:
Two slugs in a hug wild and free
Were approached by an old bumblebee.
He said with a sneer,
"You can't do that here—
This limerick is rated PG."

There was a kind cabby from Seoul
Whose car took a terrible reoul;
So the following Myundai
He bought a new Hyundai,
And since then has not missed a teoul.
(*In the style of Ogden Nash*)

In Slugville they partied with zest.
They really gave it their best.
When one slug got rude,
A battle ensued,
And the party became a slugfest.

Bill, May 1990:
There once was a Michigan pastor
Whose lim'ricks came faster and faster.
But as his pen scribbled
His chess game dribbled.
Approaching the brink of disaster.

Jim, May 1990:
I confess, of lim'ricks I'm fonder.
With chess, my mind starts to wander.
This Michigan pastor
Would much rather master
The art of the double entendre.

Just imagine how long I have known ya,
And I probably needed to phone ya,
To warn you in person
The limericks will worsen—
You'd expect that a "ham" makes bologna.

To my brother who writes from Virginia:
I didn't know that you had it within ya
To author such trivia—
The credit I give ya.
So long, bye for now, Abyssinia!

The Great Limerick War has begun,
And it promises more than just fun.
You don't stand a chance.
I'll beat off your pants—
The score being seven to one.

Bill, June 1990:
I'm more than eager to dabble
In crossword puzzles and Scrabble.
Lim'ricks? Alright,
I'm delighted to fight
With recreational babble.

But if word-war you choose
You'll be chanting the blues.
Elocution, you see,
Is a paycheck to me.
In sum, you are destined to lose

It could be phenomenal fun—
This family is built on the pun,
And even a marriage
Promotes verbal miscarriage
From in-laws, daughters, and son.

So this offer's intended
For the Hoffers, extended,
And a Sinyard or two
May join the milieu,
i.e., the clan, as amended.

First, a new rule in the mix:
What counts are grammatical tricks.
Numbers don't matter—
The goal's quality patter
(And this makes it seven to six).

Mom, May 1990:
This guy from St. Joe was self-centered
Because of the interest engendered.
When his verse took the prize
He had stars in his eyes,
Though his was the only one entered.

It looks like there's trouble a-brewin',
A limerick war is ensuin'.
Take it from an old pro
We'll put on a show,
And you guys won't know what you're doin'.

Bill, June 1990:
Not surprisingly, Mother has shown
That she, too, can foster a groan.
For she is the source
Of us, but of course,
She couldn't have done it alone.

And I find it a tiny bit sad
That some have not welcomed the fad.
(Can he compose
While blowing his nose?)
Oh, when will we hear from Dad?

There remains, too, a brother and sis
Who've yet to write something like this
Sooner or late
Their doomed to their fate—
A plunge down the lim'rick abyss.

For this is the family curse:
No matter how much we're adverse,
We'll waste all our time
On rhythm and rhyme.
It couldn't get much verse.

Mom, June 1990:
There was a young lady I knew,
Whether Janet or Peggy or who?
She was quite a dame—
I've forgotten her name—
But it ain't necessarily Sue.

Her fame and her fortune, it's true
Were legend among all that she knew.
A gem of a gal—
I know it's not Sal—
But it ain't necessarily Sue.

Jim, June 1990:
I see I have tickled a nerve,
And you certainly do write with verve.
I assume what we're after
Is really the laughter,
While I get the rebuke I deserve.

A problem for you, little brother:
(And it has not to do with our mother)
'Cause I don't understand
To play chess with one hand
And write all this stuff with the other.

Not one to be ever outdone,
Especially concerning the pun,
I may not write books
(Please, no dirty looks!)
But with limericks I'll have y'on the run.

You're starting to get in my hair,
Though you write with incredible flair.
I detected a stammer.
You erred in your grammar,
Confusing "there", "their", and "they're".

If quality's really the issue,
Then I warn you, you're going to wish you
Had never retorted.
This thing could get sordid.
You'd better go reach for a tissue.

How come some of yours are inverted?
True limericism you've murdered.
The acceptable way
Is A A B B A,
The meter and rhyme undisturb-ed.

Mom and Dad think to get in the act.
I'll give E for their effort, in fact.
But their two oldest sons
Are all full of puns—
Of limericks, they have the knact.

Mom's limericks are a bit sloppy—
She duplicates by carbon copy.
We'll try not to snoot her
While using computer
And storing our poems on a floppy.

We have the dubious mission
To uphold the Hoffer tradition:
The perpetual pun,
The finest bar none—
But I think Al and Den have gone fishin'.

We're starting to get awfully brave,
As fame and fortune we crave.
This war is unending.
O the stuff we are sending!
Ogden Nash would roll oe'r in his grave!

May the spirit of Ogden Nash
Arise from the dusty ash
To smile or to frown,
Thumbs up or thumbs down,
To bless or condemn this trash.

Bill, July 1990: (At this point Bill took the war to a new level. He wrote several limericks upside down, sideways, and one even in mirror image fashion.)
I'm compelled to add one more word
Or two. Lest there be a roar heard
From those who thirst
For the absolute worst.
Let us therefore stumble forward.

(Sideways left):
Your glorious dreams are now bereft
As we show how extraordinarily deft
The words may spill
From brother Bill.
For you, mere surrender is left.

(Sideways right):
We now advance the sibling fight
To a dizzying, daring, frightful height
To prove the contention—
The art of invention
Is ours—we demonstrate we are right.

(Upside down):
We take liberty in flirting
With rules, knowingly perverting.
And thus we compute
A fresh-charted route,
Our priceless text inverting.

(In the middle of the above verses):
Sweet, little
Poetic drivel
Can rhyme
Half-time
Here in the middle.

(And on the back of the page, in mirror image):

   —The flip side is really perverse—
   To read, you may have to rehearse.
        You'll find it clearer
        To read in a mirror,
   'Cause the finale is done in reverse.

Jim, July 1990:
I don't know how long I can stand it,
Yet replies such as yours do demand it.
Your neat "turns of phrase"
Are deserving of praise—
I will now have to work like a bandit.

Some folks show themselves very sage
By writing all over the page.
But 'tis not the seasoning
For circular reasoning—
So the war we'll continue to rage.

You are sending such obvious bunkle,
And you think you have found a new wrunkle.
You will writhe, you will scream,
Awful nightmares you'll dream.
No way am I gonna cry "uncle".

Here comes the grand coup de grace.
A new thing I throw in your face.
You cannot beat him,
He's trilingual Jim,
Intent on Bill's utter disgrace.

Que dejes poesía a mi cargo,
Porque puedo escribir tiempo largo
En idiomas así
Desconocidos por ti;
Tratarás de competir, sin embargo.

Mereces bastante alabanzas,
Y parece que nunca te cansas.
Mas te sale en vano
Lo que escribes a mano,
Porque nunca a mí me alcanzas.

Meu conselho vai cair meio duro;
Nós poetas preferimos ar puro.
Mas o lixo que escreve
Tem um cheiro não leve,
E é digno de ficar no escuro.

Bill, December 1990:
'Twas a couple weeks before Christmas,
And all over my desk
Was a gargantuan, brobdignagian,
Grinch-inspiring mess.

The children were nestled
All snug by the screen,
From whence visions of capitalism
Oozed like whipped cream.

In a rare moment to ponder
My eye chanced to wander
'Pon a faded, forgotten page.
I succumbed to rage:

Thoughts of work vanish,
This one's in Spanish—
Or is it Portuguese?
And I, forced to seize
My pen.
And then . . .

(Quoth Edward Lear,
"Never fear!")

. . . What to my exhausted brain should appear
But a miniature epic, a Christmas cheer.

Oh, Rudolph, with your nose so runny,
Help me write some lines so funny,
Infused with subtle, clever tricks
That need not pose as limericks.

Let pen on the crest of the blank-white page
Compose the phrase so glittering and sage!
(We pause for a question in the midst of our play:
Are you sure Dr. Seuss started this way?)

Of a sudden, on the floor,
There was old Saint Exodor.*
He was dressed in black fur from his head to his toe,
And his red bandana emitted a glow.

He wagged his tail in doggy delight
To tell me it would be alright.
Then, placing a forepaw under his belly,
He lumbered over in front of the telly.

The kids all screamed, "Get out of the way!"
But Exodor said, "I have something to say."
He took his time, in big dog fashion,
But the words came out with warmth and passion:

"Merry Christmas to Mom, Dad, Jim, Vera, Alice, Mike, and Den.
Peace on earth, good will toward men."

———————
*Bill's dog, a German shepherd/sheepdog mix, with perhaps some other critters mixed in.

Also by James Hoffer, *Secrets and Mysteries of the Lost Ark: A Bible Adventure*. Available in four languages (English, Spanish, Portuguese, and French), it is an in-depth Bible study on the topic of the ancient Jewish sanctuary and its far-reaching prophetic significance. Please order your copy from our publisher, TEACH Services, 1-800-367-1844.

Visit our website for helpful videos and teaching aids, or to order an autographed copy of either of our English books:

https://LostArkSeminar.com

Our books are also available in print or electronic versions at Amazon or Barnes and Noble.

We invite you to view the complete
selection of titles we publish at:
www.ASPECTBooks.com

We encourage you to write us
with your thoughts about this,
or any other book we publish at:
info@ASPECTBooks.com

ASPECT Books' titles may be purchased in
bulk quantities for educational, fund-raising,
business, or promotional use.
bulksales@ASPECTBooks.com

Finally, if you are interested in seeing
your own book in print, please contact us at:
publishing@ASPECTBooks.com

We are happy to review your manuscript at no charge.

www.ingramcontent.com/pod-product-compliance
Lightning Source LLC
Chambersburg PA
CBHW071850230426
43671CB00012B/2127